book of mormon

big picture/little picture
STUDY GUIDE

by Cali Black
creator of @comefollowmestudy

what to expect

Hey! I am SO glad that you are here.

I love the scriptures, and I love feeling confident while I read. When I used to try to "study the scriptures", I would often feel confused, and I didn't really have a great experience. I felt like everyone else "got it", and I was stuck with a kid-level understanding.

I've spent years trying to learn about the background info for all of these intricate scripture stories. I've learned about people, symbolism, cultural differences, and facts galore.

But I also know that most people don't have time to read elaborate and detailed historical books in order to learn all of this for yourselves.

So I started creating study guides that were for people like me. Latter-day Saints who:
- **want to feel like they understand the scriptures more**
- **but don't have much extra time to devote to figuring it out**

As a former middle school teacher, I like to think I've mastered the art of simplification. I've taken countless hours of research and distilled them into what you REALLY need to know.

And then I realized that even more important than actually understanding what's going on in the scriptures, is figuring out how to <u>apply</u> them to my life and have them help to change me each day that I open their pages.

And thus, my Big Picture/Little Picture Study Guides were born.

The perfect mix of content, short summaries, connections, and a whole bunch of spiritual focus. I think it's a pretty good recipe.

If you've never used a Big Picture/Little Picture Study Guide, here's what to expect:

Each week, I give you EVERYTHING that you need to be successful on both ends of the scripture study spectrum: the background knowledge AND the spiritual application.

BIG PICTURE

In the Big Picture section, I give you whatever historical, contextual, or interesting knowledge I think that you'll need to totally "get" what's going on. (In simple, bullet-point form, of course.)

LITTLE PICTURE

After all that big context, we get to the nitty-gritty daily reading part.

I give a quick little reference for every single chapter that we read, including a couple of sentences about what you should know/remember BEFORE you read, and then a simple summary of WHAT you are reading in that chapter. (Just in case things get confusing!)

SPIRITUAL GUIDING QUESTIONS

This is, of course, where the rubber meets the road in WHY we study the scriptures. I've created 7 questions for you to ponder each week, so you could respond to one each day, do them all at once, or pick and choose which questions resonate with you.

Pretty much, I've packed as much info into this little study guide as I could while still keeping a conversational feel, because talking about the scriptures is super fun.

If you've been wanting to feel "in the know" before Sunday School lessons, if you've been looking for an easier way to understand the scriptures in order to teach your kids, if you've been looking to boost your knowledge before YOU stand up and teach seminary, then I believe this study guide is exactly what you need.

Above all though, never let this study guide, or anything else for that matter, separate you from getting in the actual scriptures. In fact, I hope this guide encourages you to get in the scriptures more often. Nothing is more important than you, with the Spirit, reading the word of God!

I am so excited to help orient you in the Book of Mormon this year. This final quarter is a whirlwind of timelines, flashbacks, and sad stories. But beneath the craziness there are some of the most powerful examples of conversion, faith, service, and testimony.

For ease, this study guide has been broken into quarters for the year. If you missed the January-March, April-June, or July-September study guides, you can find them on comefollowmestudy.com or on Amazon.

I love connecting with people and talking about the scriptures, so make sure you follow me on Instagram @comefollowmestudy, on Facebook.com/comefollowmestudy, or join my email list at comefollowmestudy.com. I also co-host the One Minute Scripture Study podcast wherever you listen to podcasts!

Alright, are you feeling ready?! Let's go! Happy Studying!

- Cali Black

cool features

For each week this quarter, you'll find:

General Context: These bullet points remind your brain what we studied the week before, and give you any context you need for the current reading in order to connect the story together.

Spiritual Themes: Sometimes there is so much stuff in a reading assignment that it's hard to know where to focus! That's why you'll get three spiritual themes each week to help you focus on some of the most important topics. These would be great to highlight or note in your scriptures as you actually study, or you can just keep them in mind to guide you as you read through the assigned chapters!

People to Know: This is a quick bullet point list that includes descriptions and extra info about people. Anyone that is mentioned in that week's reading gets put on the list so that you always have an easy reference, especially if you need to jog your memory on who they are. If there are also groups of people that I think are important for you to review, I will give you that info too!

Places to Know: This bullet point list gives a quick rundown of all the locations mentioned in that week's reading. Having a good grasp on where stories are taking place, and who is from where, can make a huge difference in understanding these scriptures.

Chapter Breakdowns: Often, we aren't sitting down to read the entire week's chapters in one sitting. So if you read all the general context, feel like you totally "get it", and then read one chapter. . . When you sit down to read the next day, it may have all disappeared from your brain. That's why I give you a "BEFORE YOU READ" quick reminder before every single chapter. I also give a "WHAT YOU'LL READ" with a chapter summary in case you want to double check you understood what you just read.

Spiritual Guiding Questions: This is where you get to put your own pencil to the paper and practice applying the scriptures. There are seven questions for each week, so you could ponder one each day, do them all at one time, or only focus on the questions that resonate with you. These also make great discussion questions if you are a teacher!

book of mormon map

What starts out as simply "the promised land" quickly turns into a complex civilization filled with lands, cities, and borders.

It always helps my brain to be able to keep track of locations if I can actually see them on a map.

Unfortunately, we don't have an accurate historic map of every location in the Book of Mormon.

But do you know what we do have?! The amazing Sarah Cook from Olivet Designs. She went through the entire Book of Mormon, tracked every location and their relation to each other or natural features, and created a fantastic Book of Mormon map!

You are going to want to turn back to this map over and over again as we study the Book of Mormon so you can better picture in your mind what it might have looked like to travel from one city or land to another.

And I want to add the disclaimer that this map is simply an artistic interpretation of the cities and landforms we read about. It is not meant to be compared to actual geographic locations, nor can we even come close to accuracy in distance.

Again, a huge thank you to Sarah Cook from Olivet Designs for allowing me to share this super useful map with you this year.

3 NEPHI 12 - 16

"I Am the Law, and the Light"

BIG PICTURE

How to feel confident fitting in this week's readings with the entire Book of Mormon

General Context:

- **Jesus has arrived in the Americas.** This is it! This is what the entire Book of Mormon has been leading up to. This is the "Easter story" of the New World. While we turn our attention to the beautifully profound teachings of our Savior for the next few weeks, let's start with a quick review of the greater context leading up to and surrounding this life-altering event:

- **The Book of 3 Nephi started at the same time that Jesus Christ was born in Bethlehem.** Let's do a quick review of what has happened so far in the Third Book of Nephi:

  - Undeniable signs of Christ's birth filled the land, just as prophets like Samuel the Lamanite had foretold.

  - Nephi (the Elder, who had traveled the land preaching with his brother Lehi) had passed the plates and the role of high priest to his son, Nephi.

  - The land quickly descended into chaos as the Gadianton robbers made a powerful resurgence, terrorizing both the Nephites and the Lamanites.

  - After the righteous Nephites and Lamanites teamed up to defeat the Gadianton robbers once and for all, peace and conversion to Jesus Christ spread throughout the land.

  - But almost as quickly as peace came, pride, prosperity, and division started to plague the land, leading to a complete dissolution of government.

  - Everyone split into groups of families, kindred, and friends. Nephi was still able to travel the land and have some success with preaching the word of God and performing miracles.

  - Finally, it was time for the signs of Christ's crucifixion to fill in the land. Following the destruction and chaos from the three days of darkness, many people heard a voice and eventually Jesus Christ appeared in His resurrected body to the people gathered near the temple in the land of Bountiful.

- **What has Jesus done in Bountiful so far?** He appeared, declared His divinity, and invited everyone to feel His wounds. Jesus also called Nephi and eleven others to serve as disciples, taught them about baptism, and commanded the twelve disciples to go declare His word.

- **And now we just get to listen to Jesus teach!** In all of our chapters this week, we will read the words that Jesus spoke as He stood in Bountiful. Do these teachings sound a little bit familiar though?! **What Jesus says in 3 Nephi chapters 12-14 contains almost identical teachings to what is recorded in Matthew chapters 5-7 in the New Testament!** In the Book of Matthew, chapters 5-7 contain what is commonly referred to as the Sermon on the Mount. Jesus originally gave this sermon on a mountainside near the Sea of Galilee to His apostles and other disciples who had gathered around Him. The sermon contains one of Jesus's most popular and recognizable collections of teachings for how to become more spiritually mature as a disciple of Christ.
  - To put this in perspective, even though the scriptures in Matthew seem very separated from the scriptures in 3 Nephi, they include the same exact speaker (Jesus Christ) giving the same message separated by only a brief period of time (a couple years at the most).
- **There's also a lot of references to the Law of Moses in what Christ teaches this week.** Throughout Old Testament times, which also includes everything in the Book of Mormon up to this point, prophets pointed people towards keeping the Law of Moses, which was a collection of rules that, in part, contained the commandment to sacrifice unblemished animals. In 3 Nephi 12, Jesus will mention that He has fulfilled the Law of Moses. And in 3 Nephi 15, Jesus will further clarify that He was the One who gave the Law of Moses to prophets of old, so of course He has the power to fulfill and do away with the law. This marks the dramatic transition from sacrificing animals to the commandment to sacrifice our hearts and wills to Jesus Christ.

Spiritual Themes:

Look for these themes as you read the chapters this week! Find examples in the scriptures, and ponder on what these themes can look like in your life.

- **Avoiding Hypocrisy**

- **Trusting in God's Word**

- **Christ's Love for All People**

People to Know:

- **Nephi**
  - He was the son of Nephi, the grandson of Helaman, and the person the Third Book of Nephi is named after. His father, Nephi the Elder, gave him the sacred records and then disappeared, never to be heard from again. Nephi prayed when the unbelievers gave a "deadline" for the sign of Christ's birth, and Christ told him the sign was coming that night. After Christ's birth, Nephi traveled and baptized many. When the Nephites split into tribes of families, Nephi was visited by angels daily, and preached the word of God with great power. He raised his brother from the dead. When Christ appeared, Nephi was called forth, and kissed the Lord's feet. Christ gave him power to baptize others, and called Nephi to be one of His twelve disciples. Later, Christ will ask him to bring the records he had been keeping, and include the prophecies he had omitted.

Where are We?

- **The Land Bountiful**
  - This land in the Nephite area has a temple. This is where Jesus Christ first appears to the Nephites. Later, Jesus also comes to the waters by the Land Bountiful.

LITTLE PICTURE

How to understand each chapter and apply principles to my life

- **3 Nephi 12:**
  - **Before You Read:** The previous chapter was the climax of the entire Book of Mormon, where Jesus Christ Himself appears among the Nephites at the temple in Bountiful. After being announced by God the Father, Jesus Christ descended, interacted with the crowd one by one, and gave Nephi and 11 others the authority to baptize. In this chapter, Christ begins a sermon to the people gathered near the temple. The words that He speaks in this chapter are very similar to those found in Matthew chapter 5, which contains Jesus's Sermon on the Mount.
  - **What You'll Read About:** Christ teaches the multitude gathered at the temple many different ways they can become blessed, including being baptized, believing His words, being meek, becoming pure in heart, and being peacemakers. He tells them to let their light shine before men, and teaches that He has fulfilled the Law of Moses. Christ teaches the higher form of many commandments, including loving your enemies.

- **3 Nephi 13:**
  - **Before You Read:** Christ is visiting the Nephites. He called twelve disciples and then started to teach the righteous Nephites gathered in Bountiful. Christ will continue the sermon that He started in the previous chapter. This chapter contains teachings similar to those found in Matthew chapter 6, which contains Jesus's Sermon on the Mount.
  - **What You'll Read About:** Christ teaches that we should do good deeds in secret, not to be seen by others. He teaches the Nephites how to pray with humility and gives the Lord's Prayer. He preaches about avoiding hypocrisy with forgiveness and fasting, and counsels them to lay up treasures in heaven. Christ tells the twelve disciples to minister to the people, and that God will provide for their needs.

- **3 Nephi 14:**
  - **Before You Read:** In the previous chapter, Christ taught the righteous Nephites gathered in Bountiful and gave instructions to the twelve disciples to go forth and preach. In this chapter, He will continue the sermon to the crowd that He started in chapter 12. This chapter contains teachings similar to those found in Matthew chapter 7, which contains Jesus's Sermon on the Mount.
  - **What You'll Read About:** Christ teaches about not judging others. He promises that God will give us what we need when we ask. He warns of false prophets and teaches that we can know a true prophet by their fruit. Those who hear Christ's words and do them are like a wise man who builds his house on a sturdy rock.

- **3 Nephi 15:**
  - **Before You Read:** For the past three chapters, Christ has taught the Nephites gathered in Bountiful teachings similar to those He shared in Matthew 5-7 in the Sermon on the Mount. Specifically, at the beginning of Christ's teachings to the Nephites in chapter 12, He taught that He had fulfilled the Law of Moses, which He is now going to clarify as He continues to teach the crowd.
  - **What You'll Read About:** Christ can tell that the multitude is confused about what He taught about the Law of Moses. Christ clarifies that He has fulfilled the law because He was the one who originally gave the law. He has not destroyed what previous prophets have taught about the Law of Moses by fulfilling it. He speaks to the twelve disciples and tells them that they are the "other sheep" that He had spoken of during His mortal ministry in Jerusalem.

- **3 Nephi 16:**
  - **Before You Read:** In the previous chapter, Christ clarified that He fulfilled the Law of Moses, and taught that the Nephites were His "other sheep" He had spoken of in Jerusalem. He will continue to speak specifically to the twelve disciples in this chapter.
  - **What You'll Read About:** Christ continues to speak to the disciples. He teaches that He still has other sheep He will continue to visit. Christ talks about the House of Israel and how everyone has the chance to hear the gospel and obey the commandments - Israelite and Gentile alike. He quotes a prophecy from Isaiah that this land will be the place to build Zion.

SPIRITUAL GUIDING QUESTIONS

Question: What characteristics do the "blessed" have? Which characteristic do you think is your strength? Which one would you like to improve? (3 Nephi 12:3-12)

Question: What does it look like to you to have a broken heart and a contrite spirit? How can you do better at bringing both of those to Jesus? (3 Nephi 12:19)

Question: Who is someone you could pray to feel more love for right now? What blessings and love might they need? (3 Nephi 12:43-44)

Question: How can you become more internally motivated to serve and keep the commandments? What rewards have you seen in your life from God, even when no one else has known what good you have done? (3 Nephi 13:16-18)

Question: What "fruits" or results have you seen from the devoted, righteous living of other people? What "fruits" have you seen in your own life? (3 Nephi 14:20)

Question: How have you "looked" to Christ today? How have you "endured" today? What keeps you motivated to continue looking and enduring? (3 Nephi 15:9)

Question: How have the scriptures helped bring you to a better knowledge of your Redeemer? What truths have you learned about Jesus just from the scriptures? (3 Nephi 16:4)

3 NEPHI 17 - 19

"Behold, My Joy Is Full"

BIG PICTURE

How to feel confident fitting in this week's readings with the entire Book of Mormon

General Context:

- **Ready to learn even more from Jesus Christ?!** Of course! We start in 3 Nephi 17 still on the same exact day that Jesus Christ first appeared to the Nephites. Following all the signs of Christ's death, many of the righteous Nephites who remained had gathered at the temple in the city of Bountiful. It was here that Jesus Christ first appeared. So far, He had called 12 disciples, taught the multitude teachings similar to those shared in the Sermon on the Mount, and instructed His disciples on how to preach His word.

- **This week, Christ's actions will speak louder than many of His words.** Although He tries to leave the multitude, He can sense that they want Him to stay even longer. He will perform miracles, heal people, and bless the children. He will also institute the sacrament and have the disciples administer it to the crowd. It is at this point that Jesus actually does leave the multitude and ascends back into heaven.

- **We will conclude by learning what happened the very next day.** This time, an even larger crowd gathers by the water that is near Bountiful. You'll notice that the disciples are in charge at first, dividing the crowd to teach, and then baptizing each other. But then Jesus Christ returns again and prays to the Father many times, clearly being filled with joy!

- **A "big picture" reminder that Nephi is currently serving as the high priest.** We know that his father, Nephi, had passed this role to him, as well as the duty of being the record-keeper. This younger Nephi had to witness the complete breakdown of society as both Nephites and Lamanites grew in wickedness and dissolved into groups of families and friends. Despite this chaos in the land, we also know that Nephi was still able to preach diligently, and even perform miracles, including raising his brother from the dead. This week, we will learn this brother's name: Timothy. Timothy ends up being one of Jesus Christ's disciples, too.

Spiritual Themes:

Look for these themes as you read the chapters this week! Find examples in the scriptures, and ponder on what these themes can look like in your life.

- **Jesus Healing and Performing Miracles**

- **The Significance of the Sacrament**

- **Communion with God in Prayer**

People to Know:

- **Nephi**
  - He was the son of Nephi, the grandson of Helaman, and the person the Third Book of Nephi is named after. His father, Nephi the Elder, gave him the sacred records and then disappeared, never to be heard from again. Nephi prayed when the unbelievers gave a "deadline" for the sign of Christ's birth, and Christ told him the sign was coming that night. After Christ's birth, Nephi traveled and baptized many. When the Nephites split into tribes of families, Nephi was visited by angels daily, and preached the word of God with great power. He raised his brother from the dead. When Christ appeared, Nephi was called forth, and kissed the Lord's feet. Christ gave him power to baptize others, and called Nephi to be one of His twelve disciples. Later, Christ will ask him to bring the records he had been keeping, and include the prophecies he had omitted.
- **The Twelve Disciples**
  - One of the first things Jesus did upon arriving at the temple in Bountiful was to call twelve men to serve as disciples. These men were taught and given priesthood authority from Jesus to administer the sacrament, baptize others, and give the gift of the Holy Ghost. Their names are:
    - **Nephi** (the current high priest/record-keeper and son of Nephi the Elder)
    - **Timothy** (Nephi's brother, who Nephi had previously raised from the dead)
    - **Jonas** (Nephi the Elder's grandson, either Nephi or Timothy's son)
    - **Mathoni**
    - **Mathonihah** (Mathoni's brother)
    - **Kumen**
    - **Kumenonhi**
    - **Jeremiah**
    - **Shemnon**
    - **Jonas**
    - **Zedekiah**
    - **Isaiah**

Where are We?

- **The Land Bountiful**
  - This Nephite land has a temple. This is where Jesus Christ first appears to the Nephites. Jesus also comes to the waters by the Land Bountiful.

LITTLE PICTURE

How to understand each chapter and apply principles to my life

- **3 Nephi 17:**
  - **Before You Read:** Christ has appeared among the Nephites in the land of Bountiful, and has been teaching them about His gospel and the future of the House of Israel. In this chapter, Christ will continue to interact and speak with the crowd in Bountiful.
  - **What You'll Read About:** Christ says He will give the multitude time to ponder His words overnight, but stays a little bit longer after seeing the crowd's desire for Him to continue speaking. He asks them to bring their sick and afflicted to Him, and He heals all of them. Next, He asks for all of the little children to come forward. Christ prays unspeakable words for the multitude. He is full of joy, weeps, prays again, and angels come to encircle the children.

- **3 Nephi 18:**
  - **Before You Read:** In the previous chapter, Christ healed the sick and blessed the children among the righteous Nephites gathered in Bountiful.
  - **What You'll Read About:** Christ asks His disciples to get bread and wine. He institutes and administers the sacrament to His disciples, who then administer the sacrament to the multitude. He teaches the disciples the significance of this symbolic ordinance. He tells the multitude to watch for temptation, pray in their families, and meet together often. He gives the disciples instructions on what to do if someone is unworthy to take the sacrament. Christ gives the disciples power to give the Holy Ghost, and then He ascends into heaven.

- **3 Nephi 19:**
  - **Before You Read:** In the previous chapter, Christ instituted the sacrament among the Nephites gathered in Bountiful, and gave His disciples power to give the Holy Ghost.
  - **What You'll Read About:** Jesus ascends into heaven, and word quickly spreads about Christ's visit. People travel through the night to Bountiful, hoping to see Him the following day. A very large multitude gathers and the disciples teach the people Christ's words. Nephi is baptized and then baptizes the other disciples. Christ comes again and prays for the people to have His Spirit. The disciples pray continually to Christ. Jesus goes off and prays for the multitude two more times. He praises their great faith.

SPIRITUAL GUIDING QUESTIONS

Question: Why do you think Christ heals? In what ways has He healed you before?
(3 Nephi 17:9-10)

Question: Why do you think Christ took extra time and gave extra blessings to the children?
When has a child taught you a spiritual lesson? (3 Nephi 17:21-34)

Question: What stands out to you as you read Christ describing the purpose of the sacrament?
How can you improve your sacrament experience? (3 Nephi 18:5-11)

Question: How did Jesus encourage His disciples to avoid temptation? How has this advice helped you personally? (3 Nephi 18:18-22)

Question: What sacrifices did people make to be where Jesus was? What sacrifices have you made to be near Jesus, especially in the House of the Lord? (3 Nephi 19:1-3)

Question: What words did the twelve disciples teach to the people? What can you learn from this about the current messages apostles are teaching? (3 Nephi 19:7-8)

Question: As you read through the many different prayers in this chapter, which words or phrases stand out to you? How can you make your prayers even more sincere or meaningful? (3 Nephi 19:17-36)

3 NEPHI 20 - 26

"Ye Are the Children of the Covenant"

BIG PICTURE

How to feel confident fitting in this week's readings with the entire Book of Mormon

General Context:

- **It is still Jesus Christ's second day with the Nephites in Bountiful, and He is ready to do some teaching.** You'll remember that on Christ's first day at the temple in Bountiful, He had called Nephi (the current high priest) and 11 others to be His disciples. He had also instituted the sacrament, administered it to His 12 disciples, and then commanded the disciples to administer the sacrament to the entire multitude. After Christ had ascended into heaven on that first day, word traveled fast that He would appear again in Bountiful the next day, drawing in a huge group of people who traveled through the night to see Him. This means that there is now a large portion of the multitude in Bountiful on this second day who have NOT partaken of the sacrament yet.

- **Previously, on this second day,** the 12 disciples were baptized, taught the multitude what Jesus had taught them on the first day, and then Christ appeared. Christ taught and prayed many times, completely filled with joy.

- **We pick up this week's readings still on that second day, but now our focus will shift to Jesus Christ's teachings and prophecies.** You'll notice that Jesus talks a lot about the gathering of Israel, emphasizes ancient teachings that show who God the Father and Jesus Christ really are, and invites them to study the prophecies on their own. Plus, we will see the people who had not yet taken the sacrament get their opportunity to partake as the 12 disciples administer the sacred ordinance again.

- **Although Jesus does speak and prophesy in His own words this week, there are many times when He stops to quote the prophets Isaiah or Malachi.** The Nephites had Isaiah's teachings already. We know this from the other Book of Mormon prophets, such as Nephi and Jacob, who have quoted from Isaiah over the previous 600 years of history. However, they did not have Malachi's teachings. So when Jesus quotes Malachi to the disciples, He asks them to write down what Malachi said, so that they can add it to their own records. Here is what Jesus quotes this week:

- In **3 Nephi 20:36-45,** Jesus quotes **Isaiah 52:1-15**
- In **3 Nephi 21:29,** Jesus quotes **Isaiah 52:11-12**
- In **3 Nephi 22:1-17,** Jesus quotes **Isaiah 54:1-17**
- In **3 Nephi 24:1-18,** Jesus quotes **Malachi 3:1-18**
- In **3 Nephi 24:1-6,** Jesus quotes **Malachi 4:1-6**

- **Speaking of the importance of scriptures and keeping records, it's important to remember that Nephi (son of Nephi the Elder, grandson of Helaman the Younger, great-grandson of Helaman the Elder) is the current high priest and record-keeper.** Ever since Alma the Elder received the records from King Mosiah, the role of high priest over the church, the role of record-keeper, and the associated relics (Liahona, interpreters, Laban's sword...) had been passed from father to son. King Mosiah had gotten the records and relics from his father, Benjamin, who had received the records from Amaleki. And Amaleki was at the end of a long line of father-son record-keepers (including Omni and Enos) that started with Jacob. And who was Jacob? Nephi's brother! So starting from the original Nephi record-keeper over 600 years prior to the chapters we are studying this week, these sacred records and relics had been passed through many generations to end up in the current high priest Nephi's possession.

Spiritual Themes:

Look for these themes as you read the chapters this week! Find examples in the scriptures, and ponder on what these themes can look like in your life.

- **The Gathering of Israel**

- **God's Endless Mercy**

- **The Importance of Records**

People to Know:

- **Nephi**
  - He was the son of Nephi, the grandson of Helaman, and the person the Third Book of Nephi is named after. His father, Nephi the Elder, gave him the sacred records and then disappeared, never to be heard from again. Nephi prayed when the unbelievers gave a "deadline" for the sign of Christ's birth, and Christ told him the sign was coming that night. After Christ's birth, Nephi traveled and baptized many. When the Nephites split into tribes of families, Nephi was visited by angels daily, and preached the word of God with great power. He raised his brother from the dead. When Christ appeared, Nephi was called forth, and kissed the Lord's feet. Christ gave him power to baptize others, and called Nephi to be one of His twelve disciples. Christ asks Nephi to bring the records he had been keeping, and to include the prophecies he had omitted.

- **Isaiah**
  - Isaiah was a prophet in Jerusalem, the capital of Judah. He had a wife, referred to as "the prophetess", and at least 2 sons. He started his ministry during King Uzziah's reign, and ended approximately the same time as King Hezekiah. Isaiah was alive when the northern kingdom of Israel was taken captive by the Assyrians, and he also witnessed the Assyrians take over much of the southern kingdom of Judah, although Jerusalem was spared at the time. He assisted King Hezekiah by speaking with the Lord on his behalf. Tradition has Isaiah being killed with an ax during wicked King Manasseh's reign (no scriptural record of his death).

- **Malachi**
  - Malachi was a prophet in post-exile Jerusalem, meaning Jerusalem had already been destroyed, the inhabitants had been exiled in Babylon, and then everyone was finally allowed to return. Malachi's ministry was after the temple in Jerusalem had been rebuilt and rededicated, and after the walls of the city had been rebuilt and fortified. His goal was to encourage the Jews to center their lives and their hearts on the Savior.

Where are We?

- **The Land of Bountiful**
  - This Nephite land has a temple. This is where Jesus Christ first appears to the Nephites. Jesus also comes to the waters by the Land Bountiful.

LITTLE PICTURE
How to understand each chapter and apply principles to my life

- **3 Nephi 20:**
  - **Before You Read:** This is Christ's second day among the Nephites. On the previous day, Christ had instituted the sacrament and had the disciples administer it to the crowd. However, there are many more people gathered on this second day who had not received the sacrament yet. In the previous chapter, Jesus had been praying and praising the great faith that the Nephites have.
  - **What You'll Read About:** Christ administers the sacrament to His disciples again and asks them to administer it to the crowd. Christ miraculously provides the bread and wine for the ordinance. He continues to teach the group about the House of Israel and the promises of old from God. He points them to the words of Isaiah and prophesies that there will be a New Jerusalem set up to gather the House of Israel in the Americas. Christ then quotes a portion of Isaiah 52, which talks about the gathering of Israel back to Jerusalem.

- **3 Nephi 21:**
  - **Before You Read:** In the previous chapter, Christ began teaching the large group gathered in Bountiful on the second day of His visit to the Nephites. His teachings focused on prophecies of the gathering of Israel and He quoted from Isaiah.
  - **What You'll Read About:** Christ continues to preach to the multitude about the promises and warnings given to both the Gentiles and the House of Israel. He promises that when a free people are established in this land by the Gentiles, that will be a sign that the gathering of Israel will begin. Christ teaches that if they repent, they will be saved, but that they will be destroyed if they continue in their many sins. He ends the chapter referencing Isaiah 52:11-12, promising that God will prepare and protect the way to share the gospel.

- **3 Nephi 22:**
  - **Before You Read:** Christ is on His second day visiting righteous Nephites, and has been prophesying to them about the future of their land and the House of Israel. In this chapter, He will quote directly from Isaiah 54.
  - **What You'll Read About:** Christ quotes from Isaiah 54, teaching that God's covenant people have been in captivity because they have forgotten the Lord. However, even though they were separated from God for a while, the Lord will show great mercy and kindness as He fulfills His covenants. In the future, the posterity of the righteous will find peace and prosper.

- **3 Nephi 23:**
  - **Before You Read:** In the previous chapter, Christ quoted Isaiah 54, speaking of God's mercy in gathering His children. Remember that this is Christ's second day among the Nephites. Yesterday, Christ had called Nephi, who was serving as the high priest, and eleven others as His disciples.
  - **What You'll Read About:** Christ commands the multitude to search the words of Isaiah. Christ asks Nephi to bring Him the records. After reading through them, Christ notes that some of Samuel the Lamanite's prophecies were left out of the record, even though they had been fulfilled. Christ asks Nephi to fix this, and then asks the disciples to teach the people the words that He has spoken.

- **3 Nephi 24:**
  - **Before You Read:** In the previous chapter, Christ commanded the disciples to search the scriptures, and asked Nephi to correct the records to accurately reflect prophecies that had been fulfilled.
  - **What You'll Read About:** Christ requests that the words of Malachi be added to the Nephite records. He then teaches them the words of Malachi, quoting all of Malachi 3. Malachi teaches about the restoration of the gospel and the law of tithing. The Lord will judge His people based on their righteous service.

- **3 Nephi 25:**
  - **Before You Read:** In the previous chapter, Christ quoted Malachi 3. He will continue by quoting Malachi 4 in this chapter, asking the disciples to add these words to their records.
  - **What You'll Read About:** Christ continues by sharing the words of Malachi chapter 4. In it, Malachi prophesies that the wicked will be burned, and that Elijah will return to turn the hearts of the fathers to the children.

- **3 Nephi 26:**
  - **Before You Read:** In the previous chapter, Christ quoted Malachi 4. Christ has been instructing the disciples on what should be added to their records. Remember that Mormon, a few hundred years in the future, is actually the author of what we are reading as he summarizes the records that Nephi wrote.
  - **What You'll Read About:** Christ prophesies about the future, but Mormon is forbidden by the Lord to write these down in his record for us to read. Mormon tells us as the readers that Christ gave many more teachings that are not included in his summary for us. Christ ministers and heals many more people, and then ascends back into heaven. Christ continued to show Himself to the people often, administering the sacrament when He appeared. The disciples baptize and teach everyone that comes to them, and do everything that Christ commands them.

SPIRITUAL GUIDING QUESTIONS

Question: Why is it important to never stop praying in our hearts? What does it look like on a practical level for you to never cease praying? (3 Nephi 20:1)

Question: How can you "lengthen cords" and "strengthen stakes" where you currently live? What is one step you can take to strengthen your local community? (3 Nephi 22:2)

Question: What blessings have you seen in your life when you have studied the scriptures diligently? (3 Nephi 23:1)

Question: How did Nephi react when Jesus Christ asked Him to correct his record-keeping mistake? How did Jesus act when asking Nephi to change? (3 Nephi 23:11-13)

Question: Why do you think the Lord commands us to pay tithing? How has your heart been softened by paying tithing? (3 Nephi 24:10)

Question: What is one way your heart has been turned to your ancestors? How has this been a blessing in your life? (3 Nephi 25:6)

Question: When have you felt the Lord "trying" your faith? How has testing your faith ultimately strengthened it? (3 Nephi 26:11)

3 NEPHI 27 - 4 NEPHI

"There Could Not Be a Happier People"

BIG PICTURE

How to feel confident fitting in this week's readings with the entire Book of Mormon

General Context:

- **We are going to completely wrap up our records of Jesus visiting the Americas this week, and then we are going to fly through about 300 years of history.** Sound like fun?! Let's dive in!

- **We know that Jesus spent multiple days with the Nephites in Bountiful and with His 12 disciples.** He instituted the sacrament, performed miracles, shared priesthood power, baptized, and shared powerful teachings. When we start our readings this week, we will learn about the final time that we have a record of when Jesus came to visit His disciples. He is going to teach them a few more important principles, including the significance of the name of the church. He is also going to ask each of these 12 men an important question: What do they desire from Jesus before He returns to the Father? Nine of the men will answer that they hope to quickly come to live with the Lord as soon as their mortal lives are done. However, three of the men will have a very different answer:

- **Three of these Nephite disciples will ask if they can stay on the earth to help fulfill the will of the Father until Jesus Christ's second coming.** This is the same thing that John the Beloved desired of Christ, too. Mormon, who is abridging these records, shares that these three men had to undergo a physical change, or a "translation" of their bodies, so that they could avoid experiencing mortal pain or death. Mormon was also forbidden to write the names of these three Nephites.

- **As we finish up the Third Book of Nephi, let's review what events this book covered:** Simply put, the Third Book of Nephi is centered around Jesus Christ! The beginning of the book covered the signs and miracles that accompanied Christ's birth into the world, as previously prophesied by Samuel the Lamanite. Nephi, who would eventually be chosen as one of Jesus Christ's disciples, was the high priest/prophet at this time. During the time of Jesus Christ's mortal ministry in Jerusalem, Nephi witnessed the complete breakdown of his civilization as the Gadianton robbers infiltrated the government, laid siege on the land, and then saw the land split into groups of families and friends. Finally, the signs of Jesus Christ's crucifixion were given, darkness covered the land, and Jesus Christ Himself appeared in Bountiful. Jesus called 12 disciples, including Nephi, and spent various days instructing and teaching. He then gave all 12 of His disciples the opportunity to have their greatest desire granted, and Jesus ascended into heaven for the final time.

- **Now... what about the Fourth Book of Nephi?!** We've got an entire new book to start AND finish this week, and it is quite the whirlwind. The book is only one chapter long, but that singular chapter spans about 285 years - almost a third of the entire Nephite history covered in the Book of Mormon! As we zoom out and speed up, look for Mormon's observations about trends, priorities, identities, and decisions that he notices as he abridges these records.

- **Who is writing these records that Mormon is abridging in the Fourth Book of Nephi?** As you might imagine, with a history spanning almost 300 years, there needs to be more than just one original author. There are four! Here's who you'll need to know:
  - **Nephi (the one that the Fourth Book of Nephi is named after):** You know that Nephi we've been talking about for the past few weeks who was the record-keeper for the Third Book of Nephi and eventually became an original disciple of Jesus Christ? The Nephi we start with in the Fourth Book of Nephi is that Nephi's **SON**. So we start the Fourth Book of Nephi with a completely new Nephi as the record-keeper. (And, to be honest, we don't learn anything else about him!)
  - **Amos [the Elder]:** The records are then passed directly down the line to Nephi's son, Amos. We learn that Amos kept the records for 84 years.
  - **Amos [the Younger]:** Amos passes the records to his son, also named Amos. This Amos is the record-keeper when the division, pride, and wickedness start to develop in the land. He passes the records to his brother, Ammaron.
  - **Ammaron:** Ammaron is Amos the Younger's brother, so his father is Amos the Elder. He is the record-keeper when the Spirit tells him to hide the records.

- **Want to make sure you are keeping this family line straight?** With multiple fathers and sons having the same name, it can be a little tricky to remember who is who. But do you want to go back to Alma the Elder and see if you are able to keep track?! Here is a list of a direct line of fathers and sons:
  - **Alma [the Elder]:** He's the one who was a priest for King Noah but was then converted by Abinadi's preaching, secretly baptized people in the Waters of Mormon, and established the church alongside King Mosiah. His story is recorded in the Book of Mosiah.
  - **Alma [the Younger]:** He started off causing a lot of trouble for the church, but an encounter with an angel completely changed his life. He spent a little time as the first chief judge, but then devoted most of his time to preaching the gospel, sometimes with his buddy, Amulek. His story is recorded in the Book of Alma.
  - **Helaman [the Elder]:** This is the "army of Helaman" guy. He worked alongside Captain Moroni to win the great Lamanite war, keep the Ammonite sons safe, and spread the message of the gospel. His story is recorded in the Book of Alma. *He passed the records to his brother Shiblon, who then passed the records back to Helaman the Younger.

- **Helaman [the Younger]:** He famously taught his sons to "Remember that it is upon the rock of our Redeemer…that ye must build your foundation". Other than serving a brief amount of time as chief judge too, we don't learn too much about what this Helaman did. His story is recorded in the Book of Helaman.
- **Nephi [the first]:** Nephi and his brother Lehi taught together a lot, and their faces shone through the darkness when they were delivered from a jail in Lamanite territory. This Nephi also prayed on a garden tower and prophesied about the dramatic death of their current chief judge. He baptized the people who were converted by Samuel the Lamanite's preaching. His story is in the Book of Helaman.
- **Nephi [the second]:** This Nephi was the high priest when the signs of Christ's birth, and later, Christ's death, were given. He was chosen as one of Christ's 12 disciples. His story is in the Third Book of Nephi.
- **Nephi [the third]:** His records are contained in the Fourth Book of Nephi.
- **Amos [the Elder]:** His records are contained in the Fourth Book of Nephi.
- **Amos [the Younger]:** His records are contained in the Fourth Book of Nephi. *He passed the records to his brother, Ammaron, instead of to a son.

Spiritual Themes:

Look for these themes as you read the chapters this week! Find examples in the scriptures, and ponder on what these themes can look like in your life.

- **The Significance of the Name of the Church**

- **Unity and Christlike Love**

- **The Desires of our Hearts**

People to Know:

- **Nephi (the disciple)**
  - He was the son of Nephi, the grandson of Helaman, and the person the Third Book of Nephi is named after. His father, Nephi the Elder, gave him the sacred records and then disappeared, never to be heard from again. Nephi prayed when the unbelievers gave a "deadline" for the sign of Christ's birth, and Christ told him the sign was coming that night. After Christ's birth, Nephi traveled and baptized many. When the Nephites split into tribes of families, Nephi was visited by angels daily, and preached the word of God with great power. He raised his brother from the dead. When Christ appeared, Nephi was called forth, and kissed the Lord's feet. Christ gave him power to baptize others, and called Nephi to be one of His twelve disciples. Christ also asked him to bring the records he had been keeping, and include the prophecies that had been omitted.

- **Nephi**
  - This Nephi was the son of Nephi the disciple, the grandson of Nephi the Elder, and the great-grandson of Helaman. He is the Nephi that the Fourth Book of Nephi is named after. We know very little about his life, besides the fact that he took over as record-keeper after his father Nephi, the disciple of Christ, passed away. He lived during a very righteous and peaceful time, and then passed the records to his son Amos.
- **Amos [the Elder]**
  - Amos was the son of Nephi, the grandson of Nephi the disciple, and great-grandson of Nephi the Elder. Amos took over the record-keeping following his father's death. He kept the records for 84 years during a time of great peace before passing the records to his son, Amos.
- **Amos [the Younger]**
  - Amos was the son of Amos the Elder, the grandson of Nephi, and the great-grandson of Nephi the disciple. Amos was the record-keeper when a great division started in the land, turning the prevailing peace into wickedness and pride. When Amos died, he turned the records over to his brother, Ammaron.
- **Ammaron**
  - Ammaron was the son of Amos the Elder, the grandson of Nephi, and the great-grandson of Nephi the disciple. His brother was also named Amos, and that Amos had been the previous record-keeper. Ammaron took over for his brother at his brother's death, during a time of great wickedness and pride in the land. After about 15 years, Ammaron was told by the Spirit to hide the sacred records in a hill.
- **3 Nephites**
  - When Jesus Christ was about to leave His 12 disciples in the Americas for the final time, He asked each one of them what they desired the most. Three of these disciples shared the desire to stay on the earth until Jesus came the second time. They were granted their desires and their bodies were changed so that they would never die or feel physical pain while they remained on the earth. As the first few generations passed away, we learn that the prideful and wicked people in the land tried to harm and kill these three disciples.

Where are We?

- **Hill Shim**
  - While this hill is not specifically named in 4th Nephi, we will later learn that this is the name of the location where Ammaron hides the records when the Spirit tells him so. A few decades later, Mormon will get the records from this hill and begin his task of adding to, compiling, and abridging all of the sacred records.

LITTLE PICTURE

How to understand each chapter and apply principles to my life

- **3 Nephi 27:**
  - **Before You Read:** In the previous chapter, Christ finished teaching the multitude and ascended back to heaven. The disciples began baptizing and teaching anyone who came to them.
  - **What You'll Read About:** The disciples travel and baptize many people. Christ appears to them, and they ask Him what they should call the church. Christ teaches about the importance of calling the church after His name because it is Christ's church. Jesus teaches about repentance and that He came into the world to draw men unto Him. Christ commands them to write all that they have seen and heard, and He asks them to pray to the Father for anything that they need.

- **3 Nephi 28:**
  - **Before You Read:** In the previous chapter, Christ appeared to the disciples and taught them to call the church in Christ's name.
  - **What You'll Read About:** Christ asks His disciples for their greatest desire. Nine of them request to speedily come to Christ at the end of their lives. Three of them request to never taste death and to serve Christ on earth. They are caught up into heaven and hear marvelous words. The disciples all face great persecution as they preach the words of Christ for the rest of their lives, but are saved many times. Mormon writes about the three Nephite disciples who had asked to stay on the earth, and he says that they have ministered to him. Mormon explains the physical change they went through in order to avoid death.

- **3 Nephi 29:**
  - **Before You Read:** In the previous chapter, Christ granted all 12 of the disciples their greatest desires, and each of them spread the gospel throughout their lives. Jesus ascended again to heaven for the final time that we learn of. Mormon, our narrator, has been writing some of his thoughts and commentary about Christ's visit and His disciples. In this chapter, Mormon will write more of his own thoughts directed to us in the latter days.
  - **What You'll Read About:** Mormon teaches that the Book of Mormon will come forth because God fulfills His promises to the House of Israel. Mormon warns that the people who will reject the Lord's work and revelations in the latter days will be cursed.

- **3 Nephi 30:**
  - **Before You Read:** Christ completed His ministry among the Nephites, and in the previous chapter, Mormon wrote about God's promises in the latter days regarding the Book of Mormon. This is the final chapter in the Third Book of Nephi.
  - **What You'll Read About:** Mormon shares a message from Jesus Christ, calling the Gentiles to repent in the latter days.

- **4 Nephi 1:**
  - **Before You Read:** Jesus Christ's mortal visit to the Nephites has just ended. He came, established the sacrament, shared His priesthood power, and ordained 12 disciples. Nephi (you'll remember that the Third Book of Nephi is named after him) was chosen as one of the 12 disciples, and was the record-keeper. Right at the beginning of the Fourth Book of Nephi, Nephi will pass the records off to his son, Nephi. While this entire book is only one chapter, the book of 4 Nephi covers about 285 years.
  - **What You'll Read About:** The church is established everywhere in the land. There are no divisions, people are more righteous and peaceful than they have ever been, and everyone is focused on their love of God. They share everything in common amongst each other. The disciples perform miracles and cities are rebuilt. Christ's original disciples start dying naturally, and are replaced by new disciples (besides the 3 disciples who asked to stay on the earth). The records pass from Nephi (Christ's original disciple) to his son, Nephi, to his son, Amos, and to his son, Amos. As these generations pass, a small group of people decide to revolt and call themselves Lamanites. More and more division occurs, and lots of small churches start to pop up. The disciples begin to be persecuted. All of the people in the land eventually split into two main groups: Nephites and Lamanites. The Lamanites are taught hatred and wickedness. The Nephites start out being taught righteousness, but eventually their success and pride becomes their downfall. The Gadianton robbers are built back up again into full power, and eventually the Nephites and the Lamanites are both as wicked as each other. The only righteous people left are the disciples. Amos passes the records to his brother Ammaron, who is ultimately instructed by the Lord to hide the records in a hill.

SPIRITUAL GUIDING QUESTIONS

Question: What is a blessing you have noticed from either the Church's efforts or your personal efforts to use the official name of the Church of Jesus Christ more openly? (3 Nephi 27:3-9)

Question: What do you think it looks like to "endure to the end"? How can you find joy in that aspect of the doctrine of Christ? (3 Nephi 27:16-17)

Question: What did Mormon do when he didn't know the answer to something? What is a question you could follow this same pattern with? (3 Nephi 28:36-37)

Question: What covenants and promises do you see fulfilled in the Book of Mormon? (3 Nephi 29:1-9)

Question: What were some actions the people took in order to create unity in the Lord? What is one thing you could do to try to increase unity and peace in your home, family, or ward?
(4 Nephi 1:10-15)

Question: What blessings did the people have because of the lack of contention in the land? What blessings have you seen in your life when you've worked to avoid contention?
(4 Nephi 1:13-18)

Question: What was the one initial event that ended the extreme peace in the land and started the people on their path to wickedness? (4 Nephi 1:23-25)

MORMON 1-6

"I Would That I Could Persuade All ... to Repent"

BIG PICTURE

How to feel confident fitting in this week's readings with the entire Book of Mormon

General Context:

- **Are you ready to finally meet the man who has penned many of the words we have already read, and for whom this entire book of scripture is named?!** That's right, it is time to actually learn about Mormon. Remember when we read that super small book, Words of Mormon, right after the Book of Omni? Ever since this point, the words that we have been reading throughout the various books in the Book of Mormon have been Mormon's abridgment, or summary of, the events. Here's a quick overview of Mormon's involvement with this entire book of scripture:

  - **1 Nephi - Omni:** Mormon included what each original author wrote in the plates. So for example, when we read "I, Nephi..." in the First Book of Nephi, those are actually the words that the original Nephi wrote.

  - **Words of Mormon:** Mormon wrote this short connecting chapter/book to explain that he was now going to abridge the remainder of the records.

  - **Mosiah - 4 Nephi:** Mormon has been reading the records that the original authors wrote (including Alma, Helaman, Nephi the disciple, etc.) and then he has been rewriting and condensing that extensive history. This is why we find commentary like "And thus we see..." from Mormon sprinkled throughout Mosiah - 4 Nephi.

  - **Mormon:** This week, and a little bit of next week, we will get to read from Mormon himself, narrating the things that he saw with his own eyes.

- **So what is the world around Mormon like as he begins his own story?** Simply put, the Nephite and Lamanite world is in utter chaos. We start Mormon's story exactly where the Fourth Book of Nephi ended. In that Fourth Book of Nephi, we learned that following Jesus Christ's ascension into heaven, there were a few generations of extreme peace and Christlike love throughout the land. But soon, division, pride, and rebelliousness started to spread. The records had been passed from Nephi (the disciple of Christ) to his son Nephi, to his son Amos, to his son Amos, and then finally to Amos's brother Ammaron. About 15 years after Ammaron took over as record-keeper, the Lord told him to hide the records because the people were becoming so wicked.

- **This is exactly where our story picks up this week, because Ammaron needed to tell someone where he had hid the sacred records.** Ammaron chose a 10-year-old boy named Mormon. Although Mormon says he is also a descendant of the original Nephi (son of Lehi and Sariah), there doesn't seem to be a direct relation between Ammaron and young Mormon. Ammaron told Mormon that he hid the records in the Hill Shim, and that when Mormon was 24 years old, he should go get the records and then write down everything that he hears and sees in his lifetime.
- **We will study this (smaller) Book of Mormon for the next two weeks, as we read about what Mormon had to witness and endure during his own lifetime.** Spoiler alert: things do NOT go well for the Nephites. Mormon's experiences perfectly illustrate what happens when people turn away from God over and over, even when they are given many opportunities to humble themselves. Mormon will narrate the great war that began when he was only 11 years old. He will talk about being visited by Jesus Christ at age 15. He will be chosen as the main captain of the Nephite army at age 16. He will eventually find the records that Ammaron buried. After many years of war and even greater wickedness, Mormon will gather all of the Nephites together for one final battle against the Lamanites.

Spiritual Themes:

Look for these themes as you read the chapters this week! Find examples in the scriptures, and ponder on what these themes can look like in your life.

- **Standing Alone for Righteousness**

- **Pride versus Humility**

- **Listening to Personal Promptings from the Lord**

People to Know:

- **Ammaron**
  - Ammaron is the final record keeper in the direct line that started with Alma the Elder. Ammaron's father, Amos, kept the records, then Ammaron's brother, Amos, took his turn. Finally, Amos (the Younger) handed the records over to his brother, Ammaron, and Ammaron spent about 15 years in charge of keeping the sacred records. During these years, the Nephites and Lamanites experienced extreme division, wickedness, and pride. The Lord told Ammaron to hide the sacred records, so Ammaron buried them in the Hill Shim and told 10-year-old Mormon to go and retrieve them once he turned 24.

- **Mormon**
  - Mormon, a descendant of the original Nephi, was 10 years old when Ammaron told him where the sacred records were buried. At age 11, a great war started between the Nephites and the Lamanites. When Mormon was 15, Jesus Christ visited him. When Mormon was 16, he was chosen as captain over the entire Nephite army. He felt great love for the Nephites within his army, but he also knew how wicked they were. The Lord sometimes told Mormon to preach, but other times Mormon was told not to. He eventually retrieved some of the sacred records from the Hill Shim, where Ammaron had buried them. Mormon wrote the things that he was seeing and hearing around him (which comprises the little Book of Mormon we are now reading). He refused to be the chief captain for a time. At some point, Mormon compiled all of the sacred records together, abridging Mosiah through the Fourth Book of Nephi, writing Words of Mormon, and adding the original records for the First Book of Nephi through Omni. Later, Mormon took his military leadership position back. Mormon asked the Lamanite king to meet their army at Hill Cumorah where Mormon buries most of the records. The Nephite army is almost completely wiped out in a giant battle, and Mormon leaves the final records to his son, Moroni. Mormon is eventually killed by the Lamanites.
- **Aaron**
  - Aaron is the king of the Lamanites who Mormon contends with.
- **Moroni**
  - Moroni is Mormon's son. When Mormon was leading the Nephites in their final battle at Hill Cumorah, he buried some of the records in the hill but gave other records for Moroni to continue abridging and writing. When Mormon is killed by the Lamanites, Moroni works to finish the records his father had left him.

Where are We?

- **The Hill Shim**
  - This hill is where Ammaron buried the sacred records prior to his death. Ammaron told young Mormon about the location of these records, and later, when Mormon was the Nephite army captain, Mormon located and retrieved the records.
- **Cumorah**
  - Mormon, as the chief Nephite captain, wanted all of the Nephite troops and Lamanites troops to gather in this location for a great battle. Prior to the battle, Mormon buried most of the records that he had compiled, abridged, and written into a hill at Cumorah, placing the rest of the records into the hands of his son, Moroni. Following the great battle here, there were only 24 righteous Nephites left in the land.

LITTLE PICTURE

How to understand each chapter and apply principles to my life

- **Mormon 1:**
  - **Before You Read:** A LOT happened in our last book/chapter of the Fourth Book of Nephi, but we ended with a very divided, wicked land. Nephites and Lamanites alike were prideful and wicked, and Ammaron (descendant of Christ's disciple, Nephi) was commanded to hide the records he had been keeping. In this chapter, we get to finally meet Mormon, who has been abridging the records and occasionally inserting his own perspective since the Book of Mosiah.
  - **What You'll Read About:** Ammaron tells 10-year-old Mormon to get the plates that Ammaron hid in the earth once Mormon turns 24. Mormon narrates that when he was 11, he saw the start of a large war between the Nephites and Lamanites. When he was 15, the war ended but there was still wickedness throughout the land. Jesus Christ visited Mormon, and also told Mormon not to preach because of the extreme wickedness. The three Nephite disciples are taken from the land. The Gadianton robbers rise in power, and everyone starts hiding their valuables.

- **Mormon 2:**
  - **Before You Read:** In the previous chapter, a young Mormon is asked to keep track of the important things going on around him so he can write them down when he retrieves the record at age 24. Mormon is righteous, but the people around him are increasingly wicked.
  - **What You'll Read About:** At age 16, Mormon is asked to lead the Nephite troops in battle against the Lamanites. There are some great successes and some great losses as the Nephite army relies on their own strength, completely rejecting the Lord. At one point, Mormon's battles take him near where Ammaron had buried all of the records, so he gets the plates of Nephi and starts recording what he sees. Mormon thinks his troops are finally being humbled and tries to rally them to defend their families with the fear of God. However, this is short-lived, and the Nephites stay in wickedness and rebellion. The Nephites and Lamanites/Gadianton robbers eventually make a treaty.

- **Mormon 3:**
  - **Before You Read:** In the previous chapter, Mormon helped lead the wicked Nephite troops against the wicked Lamanites. They just reached a treaty, leading to temporary peace.
  - **What You'll Read About:** After 10 years of peace, the Lord allows Mormon to preach repentance to the people again, but it doesn't work. The Lamanites prepare to come to war, and Mormon leads the Nephite troops to a big victory. Unfortunately, this results in the Nephites becoming bloodthirsty and prideful, and Mormon refuses to lead them anymore. Mormon speaks directly to us who will be reading his words, warning us that we will be judged according to our actions.

- **Mormon 4:**
  - **Before You Read:** After leading the Nephites to victory and them becoming even more prideful, Mormon refused to lead their troops anymore.
  - **What You'll Read About:** Mormon narrates as the Nephites and Lamanites battle back and forth. The Lamanites start taking over cities and offering the Nephite women and children up as sacrifices to their idols. This makes the Nephites extremely angry, and they push the Lamanites back. Eventually, the tide turns completely, and the Nephites get destroyed, city after city. Mormon sees that the end is near for the Nephites, and heads back to the Hill Shim to get all of the other records that Ammaron had buried.

- **Mormon 5:**
  - **Before You Read:** In the previous chapter, the Nephites began losing their cities one by one, and Mormon knew the end was near for his people.
  - **What You'll Read About:** Mormon repents of his oath to not help the Nephites anymore, and returns to be their captain again. He leads the Nephites to hold their ground in a few cities, but eventually the Lamanites come in such great numbers that everyone who cannot run faster than the Lamanites is slaughtered. Mormon speaks directly to us, the Gentiles and the House of Israel. He knows that the records will come to us because of the promises that the Lord has made. Mormon asks us to repent so that we do not succumb to the same result as the Nephites.

- **Mormon 6:**
  - **Before You Read:** In the previous chapter, Mormon again became a commander of the Nephite army, but the Nephites were being slaughtered by the Lamanites.
  - **What You'll Read About:** Mormon writes a letter to the Lamanite king, requesting he bring all of his people to the Hill Cumorah for a final battle. Mormon gathers all the Nephites, and puts the majority of his records in the Hill Cumorah. He leaves a small portion of the records for his son, Moroni. The Lamanites come and attack. The battle is brutal, and Mormon is injured. 230,000 Nephites are killed, and only 24 Nephite soldiers remain, including Mormon's son, Moroni.

SPIRITUAL GUIDING QUESTIONS

Question: What do you think it means for someone to be spiritually "sober" and "quick to observe"? How might you better cultivate those qualities in your life? (Mormon 1:2)

Question: What is the difference between "Godly sorrow" and the sorrow that the Nephites experienced? When have you experienced both kinds of sorrow? How can you help keep your heart focused on "Godly sorrow"? (Mormon 2:12-15)

Question: What are some things that Mormon was specifically inspired to write for us? What impact do these principles have on you as you study these words? (Mormon 3:17-22)

Question: How did the Nephites manifest pride specifically in these chapters? How can you actively work to avoid these elements of pride? (Mormon 4:8)

Question: Is it generally difficult or easy for you to ask the Lord for help? How can you make this an even more natural thing to do? (Mormon 5:2)

Question: What are some of the numerous ways the Lord showed great mercy to the Nephites? (Mormon 1-6)

Question: After reading Mormon's lament, what is one lesson you could learn for how to better embrace Jesus in your life? (Mormon 6:17-22)

MORMON 7 - 9

"I Speak unto You as If Ye Were Present"

BIG PICTURE

How to feel confident fitting in this week's readings with the entire Book of Mormon

General Context:

- **We have to say goodbye to our beloved author Mormon this week.** Ever since we read the very small book of Words of Mormon many months ago, we have been reading Mormon's words as he has read, summarized, and abridged the original records prophets had written throughout multiple generations. Mormon was just a young boy when the record-keeper Ammaron told Mormon that, due to the wickedness of the people, Ammaron was commanded to bury the sacred records. Mormon was given directions that after he turned 24, he could retrieve the records. After taking command of the entire Nephite army for several years, Mormon found the records that Ammaron had hidden in the Hill Shim.

- **Mormon did a few different things when he got the sacred records, although the exact order is unknown:**
  - First, he wrote the things that he was seeing and hearing in his lifetime (this became this smaller book of **Mormon** we are studying right now).
  - He also went through the records on the large plates of Nephi that prophets and record-keepers had been writing since the days of King Benjamin. He would take these original records and then shorten and summarize them (these became the books of **Mosiah, Alma, Helaman, 3 Nephi, and 4 Nephi**).
  - He then took the original records from the small plates of Nephi, joined them to the records he had abridged, and wrote a short description that joined those two portions together (this is known as **Words of Mormon**).

- **And while Mormon was busy at work with engraving gold plates?** The entire Nephite civilization was falling to wickedness. The prophecies that prophets had been sharing for centuries were now coming true: The Nephites had become so wicked that they didn't even have a desire to turn to God when He tried to humble them. Thus, each and every single Nephite was being killed by the Lamanites, or some deserted over to the Lamanite side. Mormon spent some time as the chief captain of the Nephite armies, resigned, and then later took up the position again.

- **When we left off last week, Mormon was describing the final battle between his Nephite troops and the Lamanite troops.** Hundreds of thousands of Nephites were slain, leaving only 24 men remaining. Two of those remaining men were Mormon and his son, Moroni.

- **Despite this smaller book being named after Mormon, we actually are going to read from Moroni for the final 2 chapters of Mormon's record.** The reason is a sad one, and one that you might already be able to predict: Mormon is killed in battle by the Lamanites. Moroni, Mormon's son, takes over his dad's records and writes a few final things that he knows his father wanted him to include. So, to break down the entire Book of Mormon:
    - **Mormon** compiled 1 Nephi - Omni, wrote Words of Mormon, abridged Mosiah - 4 Nephi, and wrote Mormon chapters 1-7.
    - **Moroni** wrote Mormon chapters 8-9, abridged Ether, and wrote Moroni.

- **So this is a pretty big transition that we cover this week as Moroni now takes over as author for the remaining chapters and books that we will read in this great Book of Mormon.** Moroni does mention that 400 years have passed since Christ's birth and he clarifies that the three Nephite disciples had ministered to him and his father, but that the Lord had taken them out of their land due to wickedness. You'll also notice that Moroni talks a lot about the potential imperfections in this book, and he likes to confidently address the future readers of the book (that is us!).

Spiritual Themes:

Look for these themes as you read the chapters this week! Find examples in the scriptures, and ponder on what these themes can look like in your life.

- **The Relevance of the Book of Mormon Today**

- **God Keeps His Promises**

- **Pride in the Modern Church**

People to Know:

- **Mormon**
  - Mormon, a descendent of Nephi, was 10 years old when Ammaron told him where the sacred records were buried. At age 11, a great war started between the Nephites and the Lamanites. When Mormon was 15, Jesus Christ visited him. When Mormon was 16, he was chosen as captain over the entire Nephite army. He felt great love for the Nephites within his army, but he also knew how wicked they were. The Lord sometimes told Mormon to preach, but other times Mormon was told not to. He eventually retrieved some of the sacred records from the Hill Shim, where Ammaron had buried them. Mormon wrote the things that he was seeing and hearing around him (which comprises the little Book of Mormon we are now reading). He refuses to be the chief captain for a time. At some point, Mormon compiles all of the sacred records together, abridging Mosiah through the Fourth Book of Nephi, writing Words of Mormon, and adding the original records for the First Book of Nephi through Omni. Later, Mormon takes his military leadership position back. Mormon asks the Lamanite king to meet their army at Hill Cumorah where Mormon buries most of the records. The Nephite army is almost completely wiped out in a giant battle, and Mormon leaves the final records to his son, Moroni. Mormon is eventually killed by the Lamanites.

- **Moroni**
  - Moroni is Mormon's son. When Mormon was leading the Nephites in their final battle at Hill Cumorah, he buried some of the records in the hill but gave other records for Moroni to continue abridging and writing. When Mormon was killed by the Lamanites, Moroni worked to finish the records his father had left him. He also abridged the book of Ether that covered the Jaredite civilization, and shared his own teachings in the book of Moroni. About 1400 years after burying the final records in Hill Cumorah, Moroni appeared as an angel to the young Joseph Smith multiple times, ultimately helping Joseph retrieve the plates. Moroni also took the plates back when Joseph was done translating.

Where are We?

- **Cumorah**
  - Mormon, as the chief Nephite captain, wanted all of the Nephite troops and Lamanites troops to gather in this location for a great battle. Prior to the battle, Mormon buried most of the records that he had compiled, abridged, and written in the Hill Cumorah, placing the rest of the records into the hands of his son, Moroni. Following the great battle here, there were only 24 righteous Nephites left in the land. Moroni finished the records and buried everything in the Hill Cumorah. 1400 years later, Moroni appeared as an angel to young Joseph Smith, eventually leading him to the exact location of the gold plates and other sacred relics.

LITTLE PICTURE

How to understand each chapter and apply principles to my life

- **Mormon 7:**
  - **Before You Read:** In the previous chapter, Mormon described a brutal final battle between the Lamanites and Nephites in which all but 24 righteous Nephites were killed. These are the final words that Mormon writes in this entire record.
  - **What You'll Read About:** Mormon speaks to any of his people who survive this final battle, which includes us as modern readers. He calls on the reader to first know certain things, like the resurrection of Jesus Christ and the redemption of the world. Mormon then calls on the readers to do certain things, like repenting and being baptized.

- **Mormon 8:**
  - **Before You Read:** Mormon, the compiler of the entire record of the Book of Mormon, had just written his final words to the people who would study this record in the future. Moroni, Mormon's son, will now take over as the author and finish up his father's book.
  - **What You'll Read About:** Moroni, Mormon's son, is the new author. Moroni tells us that Mormon was killed in battle by the Lamanites, as well as literally all of his friends as family. He is alone and doesn't have much room on the plates, but he is going to write some things that his father asked him to write. Moroni talks about the importance of this book, and how the person who brings it to light in the future will be greatly blessed. Moroni has seen our day, and he speaks directly to us, mentioning the specific sins and evils we are dealing with.

- **Mormon 9:**
  - **Before You Read:** We found out in the previous chapter that Mormon had been killed, leaving his son Moroni as the lone remaining Nephite. Moroni has been writing directly to us in the latter days about the difficulties we will deal with. Moroni will finish his father's record in this chapter as we conclude this book of Mormon.
  - **What You'll Read About:** Moroni continues to share powerful messages directly to those who will read his words someday. He writes first to those who do not believe in Christ. He then teaches about the unchanging nature of God, and that He is a God of miracles. Moroni shares Christ's words about the blessings that come to those who believe in Him and share His message. Moroni urges us to be worthy in all things that we do, and apologizes for shortcomings in his written words.

SPIRITUAL GUIDING QUESTIONS

Question: Do you believe all of the things that Mormon asks us to believe? How can you strengthen your belief in one of these principles? (Mormon 7:2-7)

Question: In Mormon's final plea to us, the readers, what does he desire? What can you do to better honor one of his requests? (Mormon 7:8-10)

Question: What were Moroni's living circumstances? How do you think this could have affected his attitude or the topics that he wrote about? (Mormon 8:1-12)

Question: How is the entire Book of Mormon like light? How has it brought light into your life? (Mormon 8:16)

Question: What sins and struggles does Moroni see in our day? Which ones have you experienced or faced most recently? (Mormon 8:28-40)

Question: What evidence do you have in your life that God is unchanging, and a true God of miracles? (Mormon 9:7-20)

Question: How can you cast out your doubt, while still also not knowing the answers to everything? (Mormon 9:21)

ETHER 1 - 5

"Rend That Veil of Unbelief"

BIG PICTURE

How to feel confident fitting in this week's readings with the entire Book of Mormon

General Context:

- **Ready to learn about a completely NEW civilization?!** Before Nephites and Lamanites even existed, hundreds of years before Lehi and Sariah's family left Jerusalem, there was a completely different group of people who was led to the "promised land". That's right, it is time to learn about the great Jaredite nation.
- **If you've read the Book of Mormon in order so far, here are the references you may already be familiar with about the Jaredite nation:**
  - **In Omni 1:20-22,** we learned that when the oldest King Mosiah (King Benjamin's dad) started his reign in Zarahemla, his people discovered a man named Coriantumr, who was the lone survivor of an entire civilization. There was a large stone filled with writing on it that Mosiah was able to interpret. This is how Mosiah learned that Coriantumr's first parents had come to this land during the time of the Tower of Babel, but that eventually their entire civilization in the land north collapsed due to wickedness. Coriantumr lived in Zarahemla for about 9 months before dying.
  - **In Mosiah 8:7-12, (and Mosiah 21:25-27)** King Limhi (wicked King Noah's son) had been sending people out on search parties to find Zarahemla so that the Nephites could come rescue them from Lamanite oppression. On one such search party, Limhi had sent 43 men. Instead of finding the Nephites in Zarahemla, this search party found a land northward that had clearly once been home to a large civilization with countless buildings and rusting weapons, but was now covered with bones. They also discovered 24 gold plates covered with engravings that they could not read. King Limhi explained to the Nephites who discovered them that he desperately wanted these 24 plates translated so that he could know what happened to this civilization. The Nephites promised Limhi that once his people could escape to Zarahemla, their King Mosiah could translate them.
  - **In Mosiah 22:13-14,** King Mosiah welcomes Limhi and his people into Zarahemla, and Mosiah receives the 24 gold plates that had been discovered.

- **In Mosiah 28:11-19,** King Mosiah is able to translate these records that Limhi's people had discovered. He finds a complete history of a civilization that was ultimately destroyed. He notes that the record started all the way back at the story of Adam and Eve, and also included the people who were scattered at the Tower of Babel. King Mosiah shared these translated records with the people in Zarahemla. Mormon, who abridged the book of Mosiah, mentions that their story will be included in this book because it is "expedient" that we as the readers should know what is in that account.

- **Remember that Moroni is our author now.** He is doing exactly what his dad, Mormon, had already done with other records: abridging! Just remember that the book of Ether deals with one more layer here, because Moroni isn't reading original records and abridging them. King Mosiah had already read all the original records and translated them into the language they were familiar with. So Moroni is abridging King Mosiah's inspired translation of the Jaredite records.

- **This story starts with the Tower of Babel, right?** Well. . . our abridged version that Moroni is writing? Yes! But both King Mosiah (the original translator) and Moroni (who is reading ALL of Mosiah's translation) mention that the Jaredite records start all the way back with Adam and Eve. When Moroni is abridging the record for what we as the readers will need to know, he skips over Adam and Eve's story, as well as other earlier stories, citing the fact that he knows we will have other records of those events. Moroni chooses to start his record at the Tower of Babel, which is where we start learning about a man named Jared and his brother.

- **Does Jared's brother have a name?** Not in this book, no. There are lots of theories as to why he remains nameless in the book of Ether, including troubles Moroni may have had writing the name, Ether being a direct descendent of Jared so not mentioning the brother by name out of deference, or the brother of Jared omitting his own name out of modesty. Regardless of the reasons why we don't have the name in the record, Joseph Smith did receive modern revelation that the brother of Jared's name was Mahonri Moriancumer.

- **So, who was Ether, and why is this book named after him?** Think of Ether as the "Moroni" of his civilization. Ether was the final remaining righteous record keeper and saw the complete demise of the Jaredite nation. Ether was the last person to write and then hide the records from his civilization so that Limhi's men could later discover the plates. It's possible that Ether also abridged some of the many, many, many generations of records that his people had kept. Ether was a direct descendent of Jared, who we will read about this week. So while we won't learn about Ether's life this week, we have him to thank for preserving all of these stories about the Jaredites!

Spiritual Themes:

Look for these themes as you read the chapters this week! Find examples in the scriptures, and ponder on what these themes can look like in your life.

- **Confidence to Ask the Lord**

- **Patterns of Personal Revelation**

- **The Lord's Divine Design and Control**

People to Know:

- **Jared**
  - Jared was a man who lived during the time of the Tower of Babel. He is also a direct ancestor of Ether, the final compiler of the Jaredite records. Jared asked his brother to ask the Lord to spare them and their friends from having their languages confounded, and asked his brother to ask the Lord where they should go.
- **Brother of Jared**
  - Known through latter-day revelation as Mahonri Moriancumer, the brother of Jared was a large and mighty man, and highly favored by the Lord. He pleaded to the Lord in prayer for the things his brother asked. After being led by the Lord, their large group stayed by the sea for 4 years until the Lord told the brother of Jared to repent for not calling upon Him. The brother of Jared built barges as the Lord directed, and asked the Lord how they would breathe and see. Jesus Christ showed Himself to the brother of Jared after being asked to touch the stones. The brother of Jared was asked to write his vision down, and given two interpreter stones.
- **Moroni**
  - Moroni is Mormon's son. When Mormon was leading the Nephites in their final battle at Hill Cumorah, he buried some of the records in the hill but gave other records for Moroni to continue abridging and writing. When Mormon was killed by the Lamanites, Moroni worked to finish the records his father had left him. He also abridged the book of Ether that covered the Jaredite civilization, and shared his own teachings in the book of Moroni. About 1400 years after burying the final records in the Hill Cumorah, Moroni appeared as an angel to the young Joseph Smith multiple times, ultimately helping Joseph retrieve the plates. Moroni also took the plates back when Joseph was done translating.

Where are We?

- **Tower of Babel**
  - As described in the book of Genesis, the people in this location wanted to build a city/tower as tall as they could. The Lord decided to confound and change everyone's language, also scattering them across the earth. It is here that Jared asks his brother to plead with the Lord to keep their family and friends' languages the same so that they could still communicate.
- **Valley of Nimrod**
  - This fertile valley is where Jared, Jared's brother, their families, and their friends gathered with their supplies for the journey ahead. Fun connection: In Ether 2:1, we learn that the valley was named after Nimrod, who was a mighty hunter. In the book of Genesis, we learn that Noah (yes, the one with the ark) had a great-grandson named Nimrod who was a mighty hunter and a king in the area where the Tower of Babel was built.
- **Moriancumer**
  - This place by a great sea was where Jared and his entire group camped for four years, directly prior to sailing in their barges.

LITTLE PICTURE

How to understand each chapter and apply principles to my life

- **Ether 1:**
  - **Before You Read:** Moroni had just taken over as the record keeper following his father's death. Moroni is now taking the records that King Mosiah had translated about 500 years previously that tell the story of the mighty Jaredite nation, and abridging them into the book of Ether.
  - **What You'll Read About:** Moroni introduces the book of Ether by telling us that it is from the 24 plates that King Limhi's people found during the days of King Mosiah. Even though these 24 plates included very ancient history, Moroni starts abridging the plates from the time of the Tower of Babel. He establishes a genealogy from the last author of the records, Ether, back to a man named Jared, who lived at the time of the Tower of Babel. Jared asks his brother to cry unto the Lord to ask that their languages, along with their friends' and family's languages, not be confounded. The Lord has compassion and allows them to keep the same language, while also directing them to gather their flocks and be prepared for the start of a great new nation.

- **Ether 2:**
  - **Before You Read:** In the previous chapter, we began Moroni's abridgement of the record of the people of Jared. The Lord told Jared's brother to prepare himself, his family and friends to start a new nation after sparing them from their languages being confounded.
  - **What You'll Read About:** The Lord, in a cloud, leads Jared, Jared's brother, their friends, and their families through a valley, across a small sea, and to a seashore where they live for 4 years. The Lord appears to the brother of Jared, commands him to repent, and asks him to build the same "barges" or ships he had previously built to cross a smaller sea. The brother of Jared gets to work, and asks how they will breathe or see in the barges. The Lord tells him to cut holes in the top and bottom to breathe, and asks him what he thinks they should do in order to have light.

- **Ether 3:**
  - **Before You Read:** In the previous chapter, the Lord was instructing the brother of Jared as he prepared to travel across the ocean to a new land with a group of his family and friends. The Lord had just asked the brother of Jared what he thinks they should do to have light in the barges they've built for the journey.
  - **What You'll Read About:** The brother of Jared presents his plan to the Lord for how to get light into the barges. The brother of Jared asks the Lord to touch 16 stones so they can give light. After seeing the Lord's finger touch the stones, the brother of Jared asks to see the Lord, and Jesus Christ shows Himself to the brother of Jared. He gives the brother of Jared two interpreter stones to seal up with the record that he would write.

- **Ether 4:**
  - **Before You Read:** In the previous chapter, the brother of Jared saw Jesus Christ and received interpreters he was commanded to seal up.
  - **What You'll Read About:** The Lord tells the brother of Jared to write everything down, but He doesn't want anyone to read it until after He comes to the earth. Moroni explains that this is why King Mosiah didn't share the records publicly after he interpreted them. Now that Christ had appeared to the people in the Americas, it was okay to share the record, although Moroni is about to seal up the records again along with the interpreters. Moroni shares Christ's promises and warnings to him.

- **Ether 5:**
  - **Before You Read:** Moroni has been abridging the record of the brother of Jared, but in the previous chapter explained that the record will be sealed. Moroni also shared some of Christ's words to him.
  - **What You'll Read About:** Moroni seals up part of the Jaredite record, and tells us three witnesses will be able to see the plates someday.

SPIRITUAL GUIDING QUESTIONS

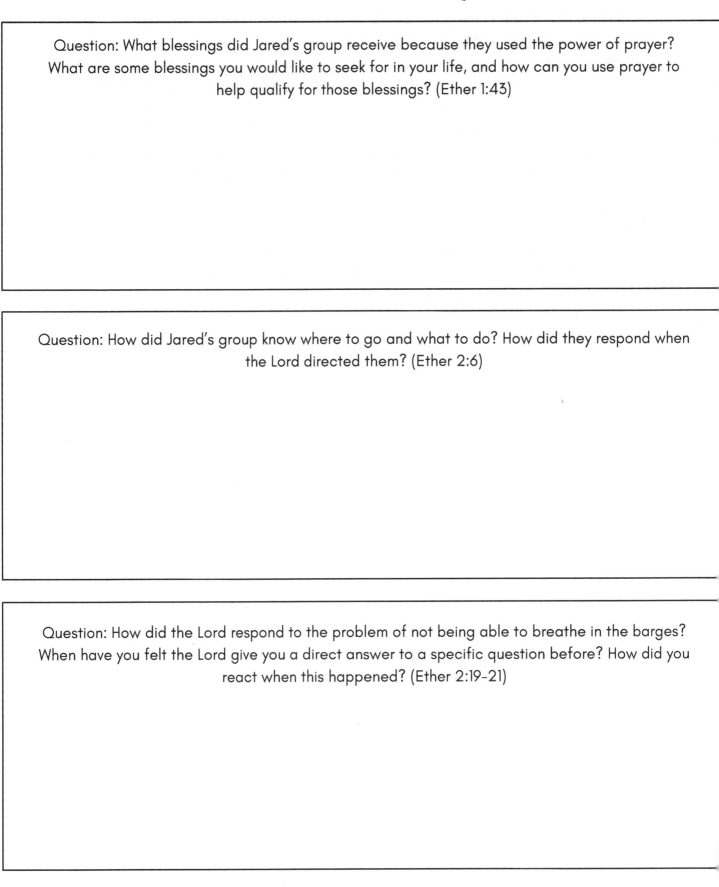

Question: What blessings did Jared's group receive because they used the power of prayer? What are some blessings you would like to seek for in your life, and how can you use prayer to help qualify for those blessings? (Ether 1:43)

Question: How did Jared's group know where to go and what to do? How did they respond when the Lord directed them? (Ether 2:6)

Question: How did the Lord respond to the problem of not being able to breathe in the barges? When have you felt the Lord give you a direct answer to a specific question before? How did you react when this happened? (Ether 2:19-21)

Question: How did the Lord respond to the problem of darkness in the barges? What are other scriptural examples of when the Lord has done something similar? Can you think of any experiences in your life where the Lord has responded similarly? (Ether 2:22-3:5)

Question: Why was the brother of Jared able to see the Lord? Why did the Lord show Himself to the brother of Jared? (Ether 3:9-15)

Question: How has the Lord persuaded you to do more good? How can you help lead others to do more good? (Ether 4:11-12)

Question: Why do you think the Lord likes to reveal things to three witnesses? How have witnesses of miracles/events/items been helpful to building your testimony? (Ether 5:3-4)

ETHER 6 - 11

"That Evil May Be Done Away"

BIG PICTURE

How to feel confident fitting in this week's readings with the entire Book of Mormon

General Context:

- **We are going to cruise through almost the entirety of Jaredite history this week, so buckle up.** Heads up that there are SO many people and generations named this week. I'll help you keep track of the most important people, betrayals, imprisonments, and places as we zoom all the way from Jared and his brother making that initial journey to the final record keeper of the civilization, Ether.

- **We start with Jared, Jared's brother, their families, and their friends entering barges and being carried across the sea.** We learned last week that this group was at the Tower of Babel at the time when the Lord confounded everyone's languages. However, the brother of Jared had great favor with the Lord, and Jared asked his brother to plead with the Lord to keep their language the same. The Lord then led this group of people across small seas, through the wilderness, and on a beach for a few years before giving the brother of Jared instructions to build 8 barges.

- **In fact, the entire book of Ether has three phases:**
  - **Ether chapters 1-5** cover the initial story of Jared, his brother, and their group
  - **Ether chapters 6-11** speed through almost the entirety of the Jaredite history in the promised land
  - **Ether chapters 12-15** cover the final generation and ultimate demise of the Jaredite nation

- **Do you remember who is writing this record?** Moroni is the one writing the words that we are reading. Picture Moroni as the lone surviving Nephite following the death of his father, Mormon. While his father had done the majority of the work compiling the entire Book of Mormon, Moroni was spending his final days finishing up his dad's record. The stories we read in the book of Ether originally come from 24 gold plates that a group of King Limhi's men discovered in a desolate land. King Mosiah translated those 24 gold plates, revealing the history of this Jaredite civilization that had been completely destroyed. Don't forget that when Nephites first inhabited the land of Zarahemla, there was a man named Coriantumr who had a large stone filled with engravings no one could understand. Coriantumr lived in Zarahemla for 9 months before dying. Keep Coriantumr's name in mind as we continue to read the book of Ether.

- **So how long is the time period that we cover this week?** Since we don't know exact dates of the Tower of Babel and other key ancient events, it's difficult to say exactly how long this Jaredite nation lasted. However, most guesses put the duration of this civilization at around 2,000 years, give or take about 500 years. And yes, we are zooming through it all this week! Something else to keep in mind is that as you read through the lists of names in these chapters, pay attention to the difference between father/son relationships and when Moroni writes about a "descendent". There is obviously no clear way to know how many generations pass completely unnamed when Moroni skips to a descendant instead of naming direct lineage.

Spiritual Themes:

Look for these themes as you read the chapters this week! Find examples in the scriptures, and ponder on what these themes can look like in your life.

- **Prospering with the Lord**

- **Obeying the Prophets**

- **The Danger of Secret Combinations**

People to Know:

- **Jared**
  - Jared was a man who lived during the time of the Tower of Babel. He asked his brother to plead with the Lord to spare them and their friends from having their languages confounded. Once they traveled across the great sea to the promised land, he urged his brother to let them have a king. One of Jared's sons became the first king of the Jaredite nation.
- **Brother of Jared**
  - This man was large and mighty, and highly favored by the Lord. He pleaded to the Lord in prayer for the things his brother asked while living near the Tower of Babel. After being led by the Lord, their large group stayed near the sea for 4 years until the Lord told the brother of Jared to repent for not calling upon Him. The brother of Jared built barges as the Lord directed, and asked how they will breathe and see as they travel. Jesus Christ showed Himself to the brother of Jared when the brother of Jared asked Him to touch the stones. The brother of Jared was asked to write his vision down, and given two interpreter stones. In the promised land, the brother of Jared didn't want their civilization to have a king, but gave in to the pleadings of others.

- **Pagag**
  - Pagag was the oldest son of the brother of Jared who refused to be a king.
- **Orihah**
  - Orihah was the son of Jared, and the first king of the Jaredites. He was righteous. His son, Kib was the next king.
- **Kib**
  - Kib (son of Orihah) was a righteous leader, who was eventually taken captive by his son Corihor. Kib had another son named Shule who fought Corihor and restored Kib to his throne. Kib ended up turning his reign over to his son, Shule.
- **Corihor**
  - Corihor was the king Kib's son who rebelled against him. Corihor took his dad captive. Later, he battled his brother Shule and lost. Corihor eventually repented and was given some of his political power back. He had a son, Noah, who eventually rebelled against him.
- **Shule**
  - Shule was one of Kib's sons who battled his brother, Corihor, and won, giving the kingdom back to his father. Shule was soon given control of the kingdom from his dad until his nephew, Noah (Corihor's son) captured him. Shule's sons rescued him and killed Noah. Shule eventually went to battle against Cohor (Noah's wicked son), and won. He united the people in righteousness and they prospered. After a lengthy reign, Shule turned the kingdom over to his son, Omer.
- **Noah**
  - Noah was Corihor's son who rebelled against his father (after his father had repented and been given back some land) and his uncle Shule (the current king). He captured Shule but Shule's sons freed him and killed Noah. Noah left his rebellious part of the kingdom to his son, Cohor.
- **Cohor**
  - Cohor was Noah's son who took over following Noah's death. Cohor led his kingdom to battle against Shule's, but was killed. He left his rebellious part of the kingdom to his son, Nimrod.
- **Nimrod**
  - Nimrod was Cohor's son who initially took over his dad's rebellious part of the kingdom when Cohor was killed. However, Nimrod ultimately decided to give the land back to Shule and unite everyone together.
- **Omer**
  - Omer was Shule's son, who reigned in righteousness. His son, Jared, put him in captivity, but he was rescued by his other sons. When Jared asked Akish to kill Omer, Omer was warned in a dream and departed to a new part of the land along with his family. Once Akish and Akish's sons destroyed most of the people in war, Omer returned as king and lived out his days in peace before passing the kingdom on to his son Emer.

- **Jared**
  - Jared (NOT the original Jared who started the entire civilization) was Omer's son, who rebelled and drew many people away with him. He battled his dad Omer, and put him in captivity, but Jared's brothers came to battle against him. Jared gave up the kingdom to his dad, but then used the plan that his daughter came up with in order to get the kingdom back, using secret combinations. When his dad Omer fled before the wicked plan could be carried out, Jared gave his daughter to Akish to marry. Eventually Akish rose in jealousy and killed Jared in order to gain power.
- **Daughter of Jared**
  - This woman was the daughter of the wicked rebeller Jared. She came up with the idea for her dad to look up the secret combinations of old in order to get their friend Akish to murder Jared's dad Omer. She danced for Akish and set the plan in motion. Akish and Jared's daughter were eventually married.
- **Akish**
  - Akish was originally a friend of King Omer. After Jared's daughter danced for him, Jared introduced secret combinations to Akish in order to get Akish to kill King Omer in return for his daughter's marriage. King Omer disappeared, so Akish married Jared's daughter without committing the murder. Akish later killed Jared in order to take the throne and rise in power. Akish starved one of his sons to death in prison out of jealousy, so Akish's other sons rose up to battle their father out of anger. This battle killed nearly everyone, including, presumably, Akish.
- **Emer**
  - Emer was the son of King Omer and took over after his father's death. Emer reigned during a time of great peace and prosperity amongst the people. Emer saw Jesus Christ. He then passed the kingdom to his son, Coriantum.
- **Coriantum**
  - Coriantum, the son of righteous King Emer, took over after his father's death and ruled in righteousness. He passed the kingdom to his son, Com.
- **Com**
  - Com, the son of Coriantum, became the next king after his father's death. Com's son, Heth, learned about the wicked combinations of old and killed Com.
- **Heth**
  - Heth, the son of Com, discovered the secret combinations of old and killed his father on the throne. The entire civilization was thrown into hard times, and Heth eventually lost his life during a great famine.
- **Shez**
  - Shez, a descendent of Heth, saw how the wickedness of Heth had driven their civilization into the ground. He tried to righteously restore the kingdom. One of his sons, also named Shez, was wicked and then killed by a robber. Shez left the kingdom to his son, Riplakish.

- **Riplakish**
  - Riplakish, Shez's son, took over the kingdom after his father's death. Riplakish did not rule in righteousness. He wasn't chaste and taxed the people for selfish reasons. His people rose up in rebellion and killed him, and his descendants were cast out of the land.
- **Morianton**
  - Morianton was one of Riplakish's descendants who was cast out. He gathered an army of outcasts, took over many cities, and eventually became the king over the land. The people liked him and they were rich, but he was not righteous. He gave the kingdom to his son, Kim.
- **Kim**
  - Kim, Morianton's son, did not reign in righteousness. He was taken into captivity by his brother, and had his son Levi while in captivity.
- **Levi**
  - Levi, Kim's son who was born in captivity, eventually fought against his captors and took over the land as the king again. He ruled in righteousness before passing the kingdom to his son, Corom.
- **Corom**
  - Corom, the son of Levi, ruled in righteousness before passing the kingdom to his son, Kish.
- **Kish**
  - Kish, the son of Corom, ruled and then passed the kingdom to his son, Lib.
- **Lib**
  - Lib, the son of Kish, was righteous and became a great hunter. He killed all the poisonous serpents that were plaguing the land. His people were industrious. He gave the kingdom to his son, Hearthom.
- **Hearthom**
  - Hearthom, the son of Lib, reigned for a time but was then taken into captivity. He spent the rest of his life in captivity before passing his role to his son, Heth.
- **Heth**
  - Heth, the son of Hearthom, lived in captivity his entire life before passing his role to his son, Aaron.
- **Aaron**
  - Aaron, the son of Heth, lived in captivity his entire life before passing his role to his son, Amnigaddah.
- **Amnigaddah**
  - Amnigaddah, the son of Aaron, lived in captivity his entire life before passing his role to his son, Corianton.
- **Corianton**
  - Corianton, the son of Amnigaddah, lived in captivity his entire life before passing his role to his son, Com.

- **Com**
  - Com, the son of Corianton, battled the king for a long time, and finally gained power over the kingdom, ending their time in captivity. Robbers were rising to power and he tried to squash their power, but was unsuccessful. Many prophets came and preached to him, and Com stayed faithful. Com gave the kingdom to his son, Shiblom.
- **Shiblom**
  - Shiblom, the son of Com, took over the kingdom. His brother rebelled against him and started putting all the prophets to death. After a great war, the people started to humble themselves before the Lord. Shiblom was killed.
- **Aha**
  - Aha ruled in much wickedness.
- **Ethem**
  - Ethem, a descendant of Aha, took over the kingdom and ruled in wickedness. The people became especially hardened. Ethem gave the kingdom to his son, Moron.
- **Moron**
  - Moron, the son of Ethem, ruled in wickedness. He dealt with rebellion and was taken into captivity, where he had his son, Coriantor.
- **Coriantor**
  - Coriantor, the son of Moron, lived in captivity his entire life. Many prophets came into the land during this time. His son was Ether.
- **Ether**
  - Ether was a prophet during the time of King Coriantumr, and he preached repentance from sun up to sun down to all the people. He spoke many prophecies about what would come in regards to Christ, the New Jerusalem, and their destruction. He lived in a cave because the people refused to listen to him, and he watched their destruction by night. He warned King Coriantumr one more time that he should repent or everyone would be destroyed, but he was rejected and escaped back to his cave. Ether saw the end of all of his people, finished the record, and hid the plates.

Where are We?

- **The Land Northward**
  - The great Jaredite nation had their rise and fall in what was known to the Nephites as the Land Northward. Various cities and other locations are briefly mentioned throughout the book of Ether. There was a narrow neck of land at the south end of their land that led into where the Nephites would eventually settle and grow their nation.

LITTLE PICTURE

How to understand each chapter and apply principles to my life

- **Ether 6:**
  - **Before You Read:** Jared and his group of family and friends have gathered together on a seashore after being spared from the Tower of Babel. They were commanded to build barges and to prepare to cross the sea.
  - **What You'll Read About:** The brother of Jared, Jared, their friends, and their families cross the great sea in their barges. Despite the obstacles, they make it to the promised land safely. They prosper and multiply in the new land. The people want a king, but none of the sons of the brother of Jared agree to be king. One son of Jared, Orihah, agrees to take the throne, and Jared and his brother die.

- **Ether 7:**
  - **Before You Read:** In the previous chapter, the group made it to the promised land and began to prosper and multiply. Jared and his brother had just died, and Jared's son Orihah became the king.
  - **What You'll Read About:** A very quick summary of a lot of history is given. Here's the gist: Orihah (son of Jared) is a righteous king. He has a son named Kib, who is also righteous. Kib has a son named Corihor, who rebels and takes his dad captive. While in captivity, Kib has another son, Shule. Shule is angry at his wicked brother, and the two brothers go to battle. Shule wins, and Kib lets his son Shule take over the kingdom. Corihor (the wicked brother) eventually repents and is given some of his power back. For a moment, everyone is united and good. However, Corihor's son named Noah rebels against his now-righteous dad and his uncle Shule. Noah captures his uncle Shule and is about to put him to death, but Shule's sons come, break him out of prison and kill Noah. While Shule reigns in one part of the land, Noah's son Cohor takes over the other portion. Prophets flood the land and Shule does what he can to protect the prophets and their messages. Shule eventually kills Cohor, Cohor's son Nimrod briefly takes over, but then Nimrod willingly chooses to give up his divided portion of the kingdom, uniting the people in righteousness and faith.

- **Ether 8:**
  - **Before You Read:** The previous chapter ended with a unified kingdom under a righteous King Shule. Prophets were allowed to teach the people, leading to repentance and general righteousness.
  - **What You'll Read About:** Shule has a son, Omer. King Omer has a son named Jared, who rebels and eventually battles his dad, taking him into captivity. Two of Jared's brothers eventually come in battle and free their dad, forcing Jared to give back the kingdom. Jared's daughter comes up with a plan for Jared to look up old secret combinations in order to get Akish, one of King Omer's friends, to kill King Omer and get the kingdom back. Moroni makes connections to the Lamanites and their secret combinations, warning us to not fall into them or we will be destroyed.

- **Ether 9:**
  - **Before You Read:** We ended the previous chapter with Akish creating a secret combination (inspired by the daughter of Jared) to murder King Omer and take the kingdom back for Jared. You will see that they're only successful with getting some of the kingdom back.
  - **What You'll Read About:** The Lord warns Omer in a dream to escape with his family, so Akish is not able to go through with the murder. Jared lets Akish marry his daughter, but Akish kills Jared and rises to the throne. Akish starves one of his sons to death in prison, so his other sons rise in battle against him. Almost everyone is killed, and Omer returns to the throne in righteousness and peace. There are a few generations of righteousness and prosperity with Emer, Coriantum, and Com. Com's son, Heth, kills Com and the people turn wicked. They are chased to the land southward by poisonous serpents and famine, and eventually repent.

- **Ether 10:**
  - **Before You Read:** The last chapter ended with the people of wicked King Heth finally humbling themselves because of poisonous serpents and famine.
  - **What You'll Read About:** King Heth died in the famine, so his only remaining descendant, Shez, becomes king and is successful in building the people back up in righteousness and industry. One of his sons, also named Shez, rebels but is killed. Another of Shez's sons, Riplakish, is wicked and taxes the people for selfish reasons. After overthrowing and killing Riplakish, the people banish his descendants. Morianton, one of those descendants, eventually comes back in battle and becomes king of the land in wickedness. The kingdom passes from generation to generation, becoming extremely righteous under Lib, and then falling to wickedness as generations of Lib's descendants live in captivity. Com finally breaks free from the captivity and eventually regains the whole kingdom, though most people are still wicked.

- **Ether 11:**
  - **Before You Read:** The last chapter ended with King Com finally restored to the throne after generations in captivity.
  - **What You'll Read About:** Many prophets come to warn the people of destruction and bring them to Christ, but the people and some kings want to kill them. Com ends his life as a righteous man. His son, Shiblom, is wicked and put many of the prophets to death. After some rebellion and captivity, the throne is passed from generation to generation. There is a rebellion from people using secret combinations, but they are squashed. Prophets continue to preach, and Ether, son of Coriantor, is born while in captivity.

SPIRITUAL GUIDING QUESTIONS

Question: What obstacles did Jared's group face as they crossed the sea? How did they conquer those difficulties? What can you learn from this? (Ether 6:4-9)

Question: How do the practices of singing and gratitude help you in your storms of life? How could you incorporate more of these into your daily routines? (Ether 6:9)

Question: Why is it often helpful to look at history in terms of a "big picture", as Moroni does in these chapters? (Ether 7-11)

Question: What were Jared's priorities and how did they affect the choices he made? How do your priorities inform your actions? (Ether 8:7-8)

Question: Simply put, what was Riplakish's biggest sin? How can you avoid falling into the temptations he leaned into? (Ether 10:5-8)

Question: What were the prophets teaching during this time? What patterns do you see from prophets both ancient and modern? (Ether 11:1-2)

Question: What do you think living in "captivity" could be a symbol for today? Have you ever felt like you have lived in captivity? How can God save you from captivity? (Ether 11:9)

ETHER 12 - 15

"By Faith All Things Are Fulfilled"

BIG PICTURE

How to feel confident fitting in this week's readings with the entire Book of Mormon

General Context:

- **Ready for the quick and complete demise of the entire Jaredite nation?** This week, we are slowing down the action to dive into what happened to one generation that completely ended their civilization. You'll remember that in the book of Ether, the first portion of the book focuses on the story of Jared, his brother, and their group leaving the Tower of Babel and beginning their journey to the promised land. The second portion then cruises through countless generations of war, captivity, righteousness, and humility. We've now arrived at the final portion as we finish up the book of Ether this week where we will zoom in on what happens with Ether, Coriantumr, and countless opponents to Coriantumr's throne.

- **So who is Ether, and why is this book named after him?** If you've been wondering for the last few chapters why the book of Ether isn't called the book of Jared (or the book of the brother of Jared...), you are not alone. However, the chapters we study this week will show that Ether is the final compiler of the records of the Jaredite nation. Picture him as the Mormon or Moroni of the Jaredite civilization: He's the final remaining righteous Jaredite alive, he is hiding in a cave afraid for his life, and he is spending his time observing, recording, and compiling. When the history of his nation comes to a brutal conclusion, we will see that Ether is the one who hides the records away, praying that the Lord will bring someone to discover them at a later date. Little did Ether know that the men from King Limhi's search party, so desperate to find the land of Zarahemla and relieve their Lamanite oppression, would discover the desolate land, find the 24 gold plates that Ether hid, and ultimately bring them to King Mosiah (the younger) for translation.

- **Want to know what I think is the craziest plot twist in the entire Book of Mormon though?!** At the end of the final chapter of Ether, Ether narrates that Coriantumr kills Shiz, and then Coriantumr, "fell to the earth, and became as if he had no life." Ether then goes out to the battlefield, records what he sees, and hides the records. It is probably safe to assume that Ether and anyone reading his record would believe that Coriantumr, the sole survivor (besides Ether) of the great Jaredite nation, dies. But wait! Now is the perfect time to go back to a scripture that might not have meant much to you the first time you read it: **Omni 1:20-23**. That's right, the people of Zarahemla, led by the older King Mosiah (Benjamin's father), FOUND CORIANTUMR! And he lived with them for about nine months before dying. There was also a stone that had some of Coriantumr's history that King Mosiah was able to translate to give them some basic information on who he was. We have no reference for how long passed between that terrible ending battle at the end of Ether 15 and between this discovery in Omni 1, but it is interesting to think about what Coriantumr might have been up to.

- **And don't forget the author of the summary that we are reading: Moroni!** Moroni is currently the lone remaining righteous Nephite in the land, over 400 years following Christ's birth. Following his father Mormon's death, Moroni is taking all of the Jaredite records and condensing them into what he feels inspired to include on the records that his father had already started. This is particularly important to remember as you study Ether 12 and 13 this week, since Moroni includes his own thoughts. You'll notice that some of the discourse in Ether 12 about faith and weaknesses that you may be familiar with are actually words that Moroni himself is writing based on a conversation that he had with the Lord.

Spiritual Themes:

Look for these themes as you read the chapters this week! Find examples in the scriptures, and ponder on what these themes can look like in your life.

- **Results of Repentance**

- **Repercussions of Anger**

- **Godly Purpose of Weaknesses**

People to Know:

- **Ether**
  - Ether was a prophet and record-keeper of the Jaredite nation. He prophesied unceasingly during King Coriantumr's reign, but was rejected by everyone. He hid himself in a cave and watched the battles amongst the Jaredites. He prophesied that if Coriantumr did not repent, Coriantumr would be the lone survivor witnessing the destruction of his entire people. Following the great final battle between Coriantumr and Shiz, Ether finished recording everything on his plates and hid them in a location where King Limhi's search party would later find them.

- **Coriantumr**
  - Coriantumr was the last king of the Jaredite nation. He was not righteous, and the people that he ruled over were wicked. The prophet Ether told Coriantumr that he needed to repent or else everyone except him would be destroyed. Coriantumr dismissed this prophecy and battled multiple opponents, watching many of his people being killed at the same time. By the time that Coriantumr was battling Shiz, his final opponent, Coriantumr remembered the prophecy from Ether and tried to call off the battles. However, due to Shiz's wickedness and the anger of all the people, the battle continued. Eventually, Coriantumr and Shiz were the only remaining people on the battlefield. Coriantumr killed Shiz, and then fainted from the loss of blood. According to Ether's perspective, Shiz had died. However, we later learn that Coriantumr survived, ultimately stumbling upon the older King Mosiah and the people in Zarahemla where he lived for nine months prior to his death.

- **Shared**
  - Shared was a man who rose up to battle Coriantumr. They had a big battle, and Shared was ultimately killed. Shared's brother, Gilead, wanted to avenge his death.

- **Gilead**
  - Following his brother Shared's death at the hand of Coriantumr, Gilead battled Coriantumr and took over the throne. His high priest later murdered him on the throne.

- **Lib**
  - Lib obtained the throne after Gilead's murder. Lib was a large man and gave Coriantumr a great battle. Coriantumr killed Lib. Lib's brother Shiz came forward to avenge his brother's blood.

- **Shiz**
  - Shiz, Lib's brother, was a man who sent great fear and terror throughout the land. He destroyed and killed with no mercy. He wanted to avenge his brother's death and pursued Coriantumr constantly, almost killing him a few times. When Coriantumr had a change of heart and wanted to surrender, Shiz said he would only accept the surrender if Coriantumr sacrificed his own life, too. Shiz and Coriantumr continued to gather all the people in the land to different sides and battle each other. Eventually, Shiz and Coriantumr were the last men standing and when Shiz fainted in battle, Coriantumr killed him.

Where are We?

- **The Land Northward**
  - The great Jaredite nation had their rise and fall in what was known to the Nephites as the Land Northward. Various cities and other locations are briefly mentioned throughout the book of Ether. There was a narrow neck of land at the south end of their land that led into where the Nephites would eventually settle and grow their nation.
    - **The Hill Ramah** mentioned is the same exact hill that the Nephites called Hill Cumorah, where Mormon and then Moroni ultimately buried all of the sacred records for a young Joseph Smith to find.

LITTLE PICTURE

How to understand each chapter and apply principles to my life

- **Ether 12:**
  - **Before You Read:** In the previous chapter, we left the Jaredites under King Coriantumr living in relative wickedness, but there were prophets preaching among them. Remember that Moroni is the author of the words we are reading.
  - **What You'll Read About:** Ether, the prophet, preaches to the king and to all the people, crying repentance and urging them to have faith. Moroni then gives a commentary, adding his testimony about faith in Jesus Christ. Moroni gives examples of faith from the Book of Mormon, and shares some experiences he has had with the Savior, including their conversations about the importance of weaknesses and charity.

- **Ether 13:**
  - **Before You Read:** In the previous chapter, the prophet Ether started to preach tirelessly throughout the land while Coriantumr was the king. Moroni, the author of this compilation, wrote about faith, weaknesses, and humility.
  - **What You'll Read About:** Moroni writes many of Ether's prophecies about Jerusalem and New Jerusalem, although the Lord stops him from writing everything that Ether saw. Ether is rejected by the people, so he goes to live in a cave and write the rest of his record as he watches his people's destruction by night. Ether is instructed to tell King Coriantumr that he needs to repent, otherwise all of the people will be killed, forcing Coriantumr to watch Ether's prophecies come true. The king doesn't repent and Ether escapes back to his cave. Coriantumr and Shared battle back and forth for a while until Shared is killed and Coriantumr is wounded.

- **Ether 14:**
  - **Before You Read:** Ether, the prophet, warns King Coriantumr to repent, otherwise he will be forced to witness the death of his entire civilization. Ether spends most of his time hiding in a cave, watching the battles by night. Coriantumr and a man named Shared had battled each other for a while, but Shared was killed, and Coriantumr was wounded.
  - **What You'll Read About:** The land is cursed, and Coriantumr battles Shared's brother, Gilead, many different times. Gilead is killed by Lib, and Coriantumr gives him battle, too. Coriantumr kills Lib, and Lib's brother Shiz rises to power and sends fear throughout the land. Shiz kills many people, including women and children, and the land stinks because there are so many dead bodies without people to bury them. Shiz and Coriantumr have a great battle where Coriantumr is severely wounded.

- **Ether 15:**
  - **Before You Read:** Shiz and Coriantumr are the final leaders, and everyone in the land has divided themselves to support one or the other. Shiz had just severely wounded Coriantumr and called off the battle for now. Remember that the prophet Ether had previously prophesied that Coriantumr needed to repent, or else he would be the lone man remaining to witness the end of his civilization. This is the final chapter in the book of Ether.
  - **What You'll Read About:** Coriantumr remembers Ether's prophecies about his people being completely destroyed if they don't repent, and asks Shiz to stop the fighting. Shiz says he will only stop if Coriantumr lets Shiz kill him, but this gets the people angry. Shiz and Coriantumr spend the next four years gathering everyone in the land to their respective sides, and the final battle begins. Coriantumr reflects that over 2 million of his people have already been killed. Eventually, only Coriantumr and Shiz remain (while Ether observes from his cave). Coriantumr kills Shiz, and then falls to the earth dead. Ether writes the final words in his record, says that it doesn't matter if the Lord will have him die naturally or if he will be translated, and then hides the records where the people of King Limhi will later find it.

SPIRITUAL GUIDING QUESTIONS

Question: What are some specific examples that Moroni shares about people who used their faith to make great things happen? Who are some of your most inspirational examples of faith that resonate the most with you? (Ether 12:10-22)

Question: What weaknesses did Moroni have? What are some of your weaknesses you are most aware of right now? How can these become a blessing in your life, even if you never completely "overcome" them? (Ether 12:27)

Question: What correlation, if any, do you see in the scriptures between people who are righteous and how they are treated by others? How can this give you strength to live your beliefs? (Ether 13:13-14)

Question: What was the curse on the land? How did that affect those living there? How can you avoid bringing this curse or sin into your life? (Ether 14:1-2)

Question: What are the roles of jealousy, anger, and revenge in these final stories? When have these emotions brought negative results in your personal life? (Ether 14)

Question: Ether states contentment with whatever his fate is. Have you ever felt a quiet peace, no matter which way your life will go? How can you seek after this peaceful confidence more often? (Ether 15:34)

Question: Reflect on the entire history of the Jaredite civilization. Which gospel principles did you learn more about? Which warnings have you taken to heart? How can you make a change in your life moving forward? (Ether 1-15)

MORONI 1-6

"To Keep Them in the Right Way"

BIG PICTURE

How to feel confident fitting in this week's readings with the entire Book of Mormon

General Context:

- **Welcome to the final book of the entire Book of Mormon!** For the next three weeks, we get to wrap up our experience diving into this powerful book by reading words that Moroni never thought he would ever write.

- **Moroni is forthcoming in saying that he thought he would have already been killed at this point.** Moroni was the only remaining righteous Nephite. He had witnessed the demise of their entire civilization, including the death of his father, Mormon. Moroni knew that his father had spent a large portion of his life compiling and abridging the records from the small and large plates of Nephi that had been passed down for generations on end. When Mormon was killed, Moroni was ready to take over. He first completed the record that his father had started (the smaller book of Mormon), then he took the Jaredite records and abridged them into the book of Ether. At the very beginning of the book of Moroni, as we will read this week, Moroni mentions that he really thought he would have been killed already. However, since he was still alive, he figured he might as well write some things that might be of worth to the future readers.

- **And did he write things that were of worth?** Besides writing some of the most powerful promises about the importance of this entire Book of Mormon, Moroni also includes some instructions for how Jesus Christ taught His 12 Nephite disciples to perform certain ordinances. Many of these wordings are the exact ones we still use in church today! Here's what ordinances you will find this week:
  - **Moroni 2:** Giving the gift of the Holy Ghost
  - **Moroni 3:** Ordination to a priesthood office
  - **Moroni 4:** Sacrament prayer on the bread
  - **Moroni 5:** Sacrament prayer on the wine/water

- **One final reminder that because of Moroni's integrity, he was spending his final days literally fleeing for his life.** The Lamanites had vowed to put every Nephite to death, unless they agreed to deny Christ. That wasn't even an option for Moroni, which meant he spent a large portion of time traveling from place to place, trying to avoid being caught. It is in this chaotic and depressing background that the inspirational book of Moroni was written.

Spiritual Themes:

Look for these themes as you read the chapters this week! Find examples in the scriptures, and ponder on what these themes can look like in your life.

- **Integrity in our Beliefs**

- **Roles of the Holy Ghost**

- **Covenants Renewed During the Sacrament**

People to Know:

- **Moroni**
  - Moroni is Mormon's son. Moroni was one of the few remaining righteous Nephites at the end of their civilization as wars spread throughout the land. After his father's death, Moroni took over as the record keeper. He first finished his father's record, and then abridged the Jaredite records into the book of Ether. Moroni ultimately became the only Nephite left, constantly running and hiding away from the Lamanites who wanted to destroy him. Surprised that he was still alive, he decided to write a few remaining records of his own. He then buried all of the records in the Hill Cumorah. Around 1400 years later, Moroni would appear as an angel to a young Joseph Smith and ultimately lead him to where Moroni had previously buried the plates. Upon the completion of Joseph Smith's translation, Joseph returned the records to Moroni.

Where are We?

- **The Land Northward**
  - The final Nephite battles took place in the area of land entirely north of where Zarahemla and all of the other Nephite cities had been, known as the "land northward". This is where Moroni is fleeing from place to place in order to keep his life as he writes his final records. Moroni will eventually bury his records in the same place (Hill Cumorah) where his father Mormon had buried the other records. This is also the general area where the entire Jaredite civilization had existed prior to their destruction.

LITTLE PICTURE

How to understand each chapter and apply principles to my life

- **Moroni 1:**
  - **Before You Read:** Our author, Moroni, is the lone remaining righteous Nephite, and has been tasked with keeping these records after the death of his father, Mormon.
  - **What You'll Read About:** Moroni finishes abridging the Jaredite records and realizes that he has more time to be able to write things that might be of value to us as the future readers. Moroni is currently wandering to stay away from the Lamanites, who would put him to death if they found him.

- **Moroni 2:**
  - **Before You Read:** In the previous chapter, Moroni explained that since he is still alive, he will write some things that may be useful to future readers of these records.
  - **What You'll Read About:** Moroni writes Christ's words to His disciples about how to give the gift of the Holy Ghost to others.

- **Moroni 3:**
  - **Before You Read:** Moroni is using these chapters to write about ordinances and procedures Christ taught the 12 Nephite disciples.
  - **What You'll Read About:** Moroni writes the words that the disciples used in order to set people apart to various callings and offices of the priesthood.

- **Moroni 4:**
  - **Before You Read:** Moroni continues to record what he thinks will be useful to us as future readers.
  - **What You'll Read About:** Moroni writes the words that Christ taught the disciples to say when blessing the bread for the sacrament.

- **Moroni 5:**
  - **Before You Read:** In the previous chapter, Moroni wrote the words Christ taught the disciples to use for the prayer on the sacrament bread.
  - **What You'll Read About:** Moroni writes the words Christ gave the disciples for the sacrament blessing on the wine.

- **Moroni 6:**
  - **Before You Read:** In the previous 4 chapters, Moroni has been sharing the instructions Christ gave the Nephite disciples on administering certain ordinances.
  - **What You'll Read About:** Moroni teaches about baptism. He talks about how the church members met together often in order to take the sacrament. They were led by the Holy Ghost. Anyone who repented could join or rejoin the church.

SPIRITUAL GUIDING QUESTIONS

Question: What evidence can you find that Moroni was firm in the faith? How can you become even more firm in your faith in Jesus Christ? (Moroni 1:2-4)

Question: List some of the roles that the Holy Spirit plays in these chapters alone. Which roles of the Spirit are ones you would like to seek after more in your life? (Moroni 2:2, 3:4, 4:3, 5:2, 6:4, 9)

Question: According to the words of the blessing, what are the main purposes for those who hold priesthood offices? (Moroni 3:3)

Question: What do the bread and wine/water represent in the sacrament? Why is it important to remember this when partaking of the sacrament? (Moroni 4:1-5:2)

Question: What prerequisites does Moroni mention for being baptized? How can you make sure you continually qualify for these prerequisites? (Moroni 6:1-3)

Question: What does it mean to you that Christ is the author and the finisher of your faith? (Moroni 6:4)

Question: What is one important reason for going to church with a large group of saints each Sunday? How can doing this help us fulfill our baptismal covenant? (Moroni 6:4-9)

MORONI 7-9

"May Christ Lift Thee Up"

BIG PICTURE

How to feel confident fitting in this week's readings with the entire Book of Mormon

General Context:

- **Surprise, we are NOT hearing from Moroni this week!** Well, technically Moroni is still the one writing the words down in the particular record that we are reading, but he is going to spend virtually all of his space in these 3 penultimate chapters quoting his father, Mormon.
  - **Moroni 7:** Moroni quotes a sermon that his father had previously given near a synagogue.
  - **Moroni 8-9:** Moroni quotes 2 epistles (letters) that his father had previously written to him.
- **Mormon had already been killed at this point, leaving Moroni as the sole righteous Nephite survivor in the land.** Moroni had already previously spent his days finishing his father's record and abridging the entire Jaredite record into the book of Ether. Despite the Lamanites trying to track down every last Nephite and either convince them to deny Christ or kill them, it was surprising to Moroni that he was still alive at this point. He spent his days running and hiding. But with his prolonged time, Moroni started compiling his own record, known as the book of Moroni. Last week, we read the ordinances that Christ had taught His 12 Nephite disciples, and this week, we will get to hear wisdom from Moroni's father, Mormon.

Spiritual Themes:

Look for these themes as you read the chapters this week! Find examples in the scriptures, and ponder on what these themes can look like in your life.

- **Charity is the Pure Love of Christ**

- **True Purpose of Baptism**

- **Wickedness Leads to Destruction**

People to Know:

- **Mormon**
  - Moroni's father Mormon had already died before Moroni wrote this particular record, but he includes many of Mormon's teachings and writings, so it's good to remember who he was. Mormon had been the leader of the Nephite armies, even as the people spiraled into wickedness. He abridged the Books of Mosiah, Alma, Helaman, 3rd Nephi, and 4th Nephi; wrote the Words of Mormon; and stuck them with the records of 1 Nephi - Omni. He wrote his own record (the small Book of Mormon) as he watched his people destroy each other. Moroni told us that his father was eventually chased down and killed after the great battle at Hill Cumorah. Because of what Moroni included in this record, we know that Mormon preached to people in the synagogue during his lifetime, and wrote his son a couple of epistles with great wisdom and advice.
- **Moroni**
  - Moroni is Mormon's son. Moroni was one of the few remaining righteous Nephites at the end of their civilization as wars spread throughout the land. After his father's death, Moroni took over as the record-keeper. He first finished his father's record, and then abridged the Jaredite records into the book of Ether. Moroni ultimately became the only Nephite left, constantly running and hiding away from the Lamanites who wanted to destroy him. Surprised that he was still alive, he decided to write a few remaining records of his own. He then buried all of the records in the Hill Cumorah. Around 1400 years later, Moroni would appear as an angel to a young Joseph Smith and ultimately lead him to where Moroni had previously buried the plates. Upon the completion of Joseph Smith's translation, Joseph returned the records to Moroni.

Where are We?

- **The Land Northward**
    - The final Nephite battles took place in the area of land entirely north of where Zarahemla and all of the other Nephite cities had been, known as the "land northward". This is where Moroni is fleeing from place to place in order to keep his life as he writes his final records. Moroni will eventually bury his records in the same place (Hill Cumorah) where his father Mormon had buried the other records. This is also the general area where the entire Jaredite civilization had existed prior to their destruction.

LITTLE PICTURE
How to understand each chapter and apply principles to my life

- **Moroni 7:**
  - **Before You Read:** Moroni just finished recording some instructions about ordinances in the church, as delivered from Christ to the 12 Nephite disciples. In this chapter, he will share a sermon from his father, Mormon, who has since died.
  - **What You'll Read About:** Moroni records words from when his father, Mormon, spoke to some Nephites at a synagogue. Mormon teaches about how our intentions behind actions matter, and that evil comes from evil, and good from good. He teaches about the light of Christ, and how to judge good from evil. Mormon testifies that miracles have not ceased, and angels still call people to repentance. He teaches about the power of faith, hope, and charity.

- **Moroni 8:**
  - **Before You Read:** In the previous chapter, Moroni recorded a sermon that his father, Mormon, gave in a synagogue years ago. In this chapter, Moroni is going to include an epistle that his father had previously written to him.
  - **What You'll Read About:** Moroni shares an epistle that his father Mormon wrote to him shortly after Moroni was called to the ministry. Mormon writes mainly about the baptism of little children, explaining that children do not need repentance or baptism because they are alive in Christ. He writes strongly against those who say little children need baptism, teaching that baptism is for those who are capable of sinning and repenting.

- **Moroni 9:**
  - **Before You Read:** Moroni had just recorded an epistle from his father Mormon all about how little children do not need to be baptized. In this chapter, he will share another epistle that his father had previously written to him.
  - **What You'll Read About:** Moroni shares another epistle that his father Mormon wrote to him. This time, Mormon details all of the terrible things the Lamanites and the Nephites have done in war. He is saddened that they became so evil in such a short amount of time. He fears that all of the people will soon be destroyed, just like the Jaredites, if they don't repent. He tells Moroni to not be saddened, but to instead have Christ lift him up.

SPIRITUAL GUIDING QUESTIONS

Question: If Mormon teaches us that we should judge, where are situations where righteous, Christlike judgment is necessary? What are some other situations where judgment wouldn't be helpful? (Moroni 7:15-20)

Question: What evidence of angels or miracles have you seen in your life? How can you try to become more attuned to the miracles of the Lord around you? (Moroni 7:27-37)

Question: What is the relationship between faith, hope, and charity? How can you better develop these traits? (Moroni 7:40-48)

Question: How does Mormon approach counseling his son in love throughout the two epistles Moroni quotes? (Moroni 8-9)

Question: Why is baptizing little children doctrinally incorrect? How does this teach you about the true purpose of repentance? (Moroni 8:8-23)

Question: What are some of the beautiful fruits of repentance? How can you develop a better habit of daily repentance? (Moroni 8:24-26)

Question: What is the final piece of advice that Mormon gives his son? What can you learn from this in your own life? (Moroni 9:25-26)

MORONI 10

"Come unto Christ, and Be Perfected in Him"

BIG PICTURE

How to feel confident fitting in this week's readings with the entire Book of Mormon

General Context:

- **This is it: the final chapter in the entire Book of Mormon.** Often referred to as "Moroni's promise", this chapter is unique in that Moroni is directly inviting us as the latter-day readers to ask God, with sincere intent, if the words and doctrine contained in this record are true. And Moroni directly promises us that if we do this, with humble and true intent, the Holy Ghost will manifest the truthfulness of this book to us. I want to boldly add my invitation to Moroni's, and encourage you to ask God if the Book of Mormon is true, no matter how many times you have read this book before. What a blessing it has been to dive so deeply into every single book, chapter, and verse within this book of scripture over the past year!

- **Moroni had taken over for his father, Mormon, as the record keeper of the Nephites.** Mormon had watched the beginning of the wickedness of the Nephites start to permeate the land. While he spent some time leading them to battle against the Lamanites as the Nephite captain, Mormon also spent time compiling and abridging the records from the First Book of Nephi all the way up to the small book of Mormon. After Mormon's death, Moroni had taken over. At this point, Moroni was the only righteous Nephite remaining in the land. The Lamanites were trying to track down any Nephites, forcing them to deny Christ or putting them to death. Moroni spent his time finishing his father's book of Mormon, abridging the Jaredite records into the book of Ether, and then he started his own record, the book of Moroni. Moroni was including anything he could think of that would be of worth for us as the future readers. He started with recording the procedure for and purpose of some ordinances in the church. Then he recorded meaningful sermons and epistles his father had given before his death. Now, we are ready to read Moroni's final words.

- **So, what next? Moroni shares that 420 years have passed away from the time that Christ was born.** Mormon had already buried many of the records in a hill called Hill Cumorah. Moroni, upon the completion of his record, added everything that he had written to that hiding place on the hill. While we don't know how Moroni's mortal life ended, we do know that around 1400 years later, Moroni was able to appear to a young Joseph Smith in angel form and teach him about this ancient record. Following three years of repeated teaching from this angel Moroni, Joseph was finally able to acquire the plates. Once Joseph was finished with translating all of the Book of Mormon, Joseph returned the plates to Moroni.

Spiritual Themes:

Look for these themes as you read the chapters this week! Find examples in the scriptures, and ponder on what these themes can look like in your life.

- **The Truthfulness of the Book of Mormon**

- **Spiritual Gifts**

- **Be Perfected in Christ**

People to Know:

- **Moroni**
  - Moroni is Mormon's son. Moroni was one of the few remaining righteous Nephites at the end of their civilization as wars spread throughout the land. After his father's death, Moroni took over as the record-keeper. He first finished his father's record, and then abridged the Jaredite records into the book of Ether. Moroni ultimately became the only Nephite left, constantly running and hiding away from the Lamanites who wanted to destroy him. Surprised that he was still alive, he decided to write a few remaining records of his own. He then buried all of the records in the Hill Cumorah. Around 1400 years later, Moroni would appear as an angel to a young Joseph Smith and ultimately lead him to where Moroni had previously buried the plates. Upon the completion of Joseph Smith's translation, Joseph returned the records to Moroni.

Where are We?

- **The Land Northward**
  - The final Nephite battles took place in the area of land entirely north of where Zarahemla and all of the other Nephite cities had been, known as the "land northward". This is where Moroni is fleeing from place to place in order to keep his life as he writes his final records. Moroni will eventually bury his records in the same place (Hill Cumorah) where his father Mormon had buried the other records. This is also the general area where the entire Jaredite civilization had existed prior to their destruction.

LITTLE PICTURE

How to understand each chapter and apply principles to my life

- **Moroni 10:**
  - **Before You Read:** Finding himself with extra time following his abridgment of the Jaredite records, Moroni has been writing his final thoughts on the sacred records. He had just finished sharing an important sermon and two meaningful epistles that his father Mormon had given prior to his death. Moroni is now going to write his own words and conclude his record.
  - **What You'll Read About:** Moroni closes out the record with his final testimony and exhortations. 420 years have passed since Christ's birth. Moroni exhorts us, the readers, to ask God if this record is true, with real intent. He asks us to not deny our spiritual gifts from God. He invites us to come unto Christ and be perfected in him. He bids us farewell as he prepares to rest in the paradise of God.

SPIRITUAL GUIDING QUESTIONS

Question: Have you ever acted on Moroni's promise and asked God with real intent about the truthfulness of the Book of Mormon? What was your experience? (Moroni 10:3-5)

Question: What is a truth the Holy Ghost has testified to you of recently? (Moroni 10:5-7)

Question: What are some spiritual gifts that you have in your life? How have you profited from these gifts? How can you show greater gratitude for them? (Moroni 10:8-18)

Question: Why is it important to remember that Jesus Christ is constant? (Moroni 10:19)

Question: What should faith lead us to do? What is an action that your faith has led you to do in the past? What is an action your faith could help you to take? (Moroni 10:23)

Question: While not becoming perfect in this lifetime, how can you become perfected in Christ right now? (Moroni 10:30-33)

Question: What seems to be Moroni's attitude as he prepares to face God? What changes or steps can you take in your life right now as you prepare to face God? (Moroni 10:34)

Congratulations for finishing Oct - Dec in the Book of Mormon!

Ready for more scripture study resources?

Keep the momentum going!

Check comefollowmestudy.com or my social media channels @comefollowmestudy for more information on how to get other Book of Mormon Study Guides, or grab a new study guide for Doctrine and Covenants! Thank you for your continued support.

Got any questions or feedback? I'd love to hear from you at caliblack@comefollowmestudy.com.

Made in United States
Troutdale, OR
01/17/2025